ROCKFORD'S
FORGOTTEN
DRIVING PARK

RACING, POLITICS & CIRCUSES

AMANDA BECKER

THE
History
PRESS

Published by The History Press
Charleston, SC
www.historypress.net

Front cover (clockwise from top left): Fred Moffatt was a cigar store owner and is pictured with his horse Mack F. It is not known where this photograph was taken. *From the Midway Village Museum Digital Collection*; Laverne Cole and Lorena Day crossed the finish line in almost a dead heat. *From the Rockford Chamber of Commerce, 1912*; John Lawson, the "Terrible Swede." *Courtesy of Richard Arthur Norton*; Smith and Enander opened a sales and repair shop at 114 North Madison Street. Smith was a regular rider at Rockford Driving Park. *Courtesy of Michael DeBock*.

Back cover: Driving park map from the day "Speed" Bradford tried to break the speed record. *From "Map Shows How to Get to American Legion Race Today,"* Republic, *June 29, 1930*; *inset*: Rockford Motor Racing Association advertising picture. *From* Morning Star, *July 31, 1921*.

First published 2019

Manufactured in the United States

ISBN 9781467141963

Library of Congress Control Number: 2019937041

Notice: The information in this book is true and complete to the best of our knowledge. It is offered without guarantee on the part of the author or The History Press. The author and The History Press disclaim all liability in connection with the use of this book.

This book is dedicated to my family, who stressed education, and to Dr. John Molyneaux and John C. Nelson, who believed in me.

CONTENTS

ACKNOWLEDGEMENTS

*K*athi Kresol, Ben Gibson and Sara Miller guided me through the publishing process. Michael DeBlock, Richard Arthur Norton and Lois and Truman Lander allowed me to use their photographs. Lloyd Fry allowed Terri Turner and I to interview him. Ernest Stokes, Denise Williams and Dr. Catherine Forslund edited my work.

AUTHOR'S NOTE

*M*y research began in 2007, when I visited the Rockford Public Library's local history room during a teacher symposium field trip. Teresa Bartch and Terri Turner perused the Rockfordiana file and extracted the 1924 Ku Klux Klan rally program held at the driving park. We discovered that the park was located in the neighborhood of my grandfather John "Jack" Flanders. He remembered circuses being held there and brought water to the elephants for free admission. My grandfather also stated that he remembered the driving park's wrought-iron gates across Huffman Boulevard where Fulton Avenue ended. According to him, the gate was later thrown by the railroad tracks and neglected until it was discovered by a scrap dealer. I think the same thing happened to the driving park's history.

In 2010, John Molyneaux encouraged me to write articles for the Rockford Historical Society's quarterly publication, *Nuggets*. In 2013, I needed a new subject to write about. I started researching the driving park and thought I could maybe write two articles. I quickly realized that the driving park story was deeper and richer than originally thought. The basis for the first two chapters was published in the 2013 summer and fall issues of *Nuggets*. I became addicted to researching the park. I studied the area on foot, took pictures and drove the streets to confirm the park's boundaries. I even rented a metal detector to find a horseshoe or some relic from the park to have as a trophy for rediscovering its history. I only found a potential square-headed fence nail and piece of scrap metal.

The driving park was forgotten in Rockford history possibly because it was a failure—unlike Harlem Park, which was a success—or possibly because of scandals involving liquor and gambling. Or possibly it was because of its spotty existence, which saw it being used for racing one season and used as farmland the next. Or possibly it was because little to no physical evidence of the park exists. Whatever the reason for its erasure from the Rockford history files, I hope that this book helps to ensure its inclusion in the future.

1.

DEVELOPMENT OF ROCKFORD'S DRIVING PARK

Many things are remembered in Rockford history. Historians, civic leaders and citizens themselves control what is remembered and what is forgotten. One example is Harlem Park. Harlem Park is usually recognized as *the* premier park in Rockford during its lifespan. Built in 1891 and closed in 1928, it has been researched and lectured on in depth. Pictures, Lyle Baie's book *Harlem Park: The People and the Times* and many other references have been made to Harlem Park in other Rockford histories, such as *Rockford: An Illustrated History*, by John Lundin, and *Sinnissippi Saga*, which was compiled and edited by C. Hal Nelson. However, at the same time Harlem Park was open and drew crowds by the thousands, so, too, was the Rockford North End Driving Park, which was located west of Harlem Park. Harlem Park has been remembered, and the driving park has been forgotten. A search of the Rockford newspapers published at the time reveals numerous references to the park and extensive descriptions of the events held there. The citizens of Rockford would have known both parks just as well. The reasons for erasure are numerous, but the basic reason has to be rooted in the different purposes of the two parks. The driving park was built for singular events and was not steadily open season after season like Harlem Park, and it was originally a "rich adult playground," while Harlem Park was suited for people of all ages and economic backgrounds. There are numerous other reasons why the park failed to be remembered by historians, and they will appear throughout this work.

During the late 1800s, a variety of forms of mass entertainment were enjoyed by the general public. After long hours of toiling in the factories, workers enjoyed vaudeville acts, nickelodeons, baseball, public parks and a variety of festivals at which they could unwind after their ten-hour shifts and six-day workweeks. Most people simply walked to their destinations or used horses. Horses were everywhere and were used for a variety of purposes in the nineteenth century. They helped plow fields, pulled carts/ wagons and were also seen as class/status symbols. In the post–Civil War era (1865–1900), horse traffic increased as urban populations swelled. People were attracted to urban jobs, new technologies, entertainments and/or the excitement of city-dwelling. Many cities had to redesign their roadways to accommodate the rise in traffic. For example, the Bronx region of New York was designed around a "Grand Concourse," with central lanes dedicated to higher-speed drivers and outside lanes for slower delivery wagons or promenading carriages on a Sunday drive.

Industrialization increased due to immigration, innovation, tax incentives, an abundance of raw materials and cheap labor and an insatiable demand for consumer goods. As a result, during the late nineteenth century, many workers had disposable incomes they could use to buy their own horse or rent a horse and carriage for an evening out on the town. In 1852, Charles Astor Bristed wrote in his book *The Upper Ten Thousand*: "The first thing, as a general rule, that a young Gothamite does is to get a horse; the second, to get a wife." The wealthy industrialists could not only afford their own horse(s) but could also take their ownership to the next level, which involved training and then racing the horses. Members of the lower classes who could not afford to buy their own horses could aspire to one day own one by watching the races. Horse racing is a unique form of entertainment, because it is one of the few sporting events at which both the rich and poor could be seen at the same venue. In addition, it offered a chance for a drayman or milk-cart driver to prove that his horse was as swift as a well-bred steed. Rockford was no exception to these national trends. Many wealthy industrialists in town had capital and a determination to turn their ambitious dreams into reality.

There are two forms of horse racing: jockeyed (riding horseback) and harness (driving the horse from a cart). According to Robert Temple, in his book *The History of Harness Racing in New England*, "In general the public was far more receptive to harness racing than thoroughbreds. Thoroughbreds were viewed by many as a reflection of the patronizing English upper class who referred to racing as 'The Sport of Kings.'" Harness (sulky) racing has roots that date back to ancient times. Harness racetracks were called "driving parks," "trotting parks" or "speedways," because the men who raced the horses were and still are known as "drivers"—not jockeys. Originally, the sulkies (carts or wagons) that were pulled behind the horses had either two or four large wheels. The sulkies also generally lacked springs, which created more exertion for the horse. The sulky design was changed in 1892, when Bud Doble created a sulky with smaller pneumatic tires and a lower profile. The new design became the standard sulky due to its smoother ride and aerodynamics (allowing for less stress for the horse).

The Standardbred is the breed of horse used for harness racing. Standardbred horses are a combination of many different horses. In 1788, a Thoroughbred horse named Messenger was exported from England to Philadelphia. The descendants of Messenger were bred with Morgan horses in the mid-1800s to produce the American Standardbred. Standardbred horses are bred for trotting and pacing racing because they have shorter legs and a longer body than Thoroughbreds. Standardbreds are also less "high strung" than Thoroughbreds, which makes them more suitable for sulky racing because there is more strategy involved than in jockeyed racing.

Races were conducted on roads throughout the late 1700s and through the mid-1800s, until building tracks became popular and provided a safer environment for men to race their steeds. The start of the race had no starting gate, or "rolling gate," as is used today. Instead, horses trotted alongside one another on the backstretch until they came to the starting line. An official would yell "go" if the horses were evenly aligned, and the race start would be official. If not, a "false start" was generally declared by ringing a bell. Most races in the 1800s, as today, ran the length of one mile, and winning times varied between two and three minutes.

Across the nation, driving/trotting parks were built directly after the Civil War. Even President Ulysses S. Grant loved to race his horse at top speeds in Washington and was handed a speeding ticket. In 1868, Hiram S. Brown spearheaded a Rockford Driving Park Association on his property near Garrison on Rockford's northwest side. The park was touted as full of promise (a common theme for Rockford's Driving Park in the years that followed). However, this association must not have existed for any length of time, because there were only two newspaper articles that mentioned it in 1868, and none followed those two.

The fairgrounds became the most popular place for horse racing in Rockford after the Civil War. A one-third-mile track was developed in 1866, and horses trotted very tightly during the annual fairs. Since a track was already at the fairgrounds, this may explain why Brown's track did not

Fred Moffatt was a cigar store owner and is pictured with his horse Mack F. It is not known where this photograph was taken. *From the Midway Village Museum Digital Collection.*

survive. By the late 1880s, people in Rockford quickly began to conclude that the area designated for the fair had outlived its purpose, because the grounds were too small for all of the exhibits and the large crowds. A reporter for the *Rockford Daily Gazette* believed that the fairgrounds should become a "soldier's memorial park" because "Winnebago county does not lack patriotic sentiment nor gratitude to the old soldiers, but it does lack a lasting evidence of that sentiment in any visible shape." Some area residents were tired of street closures, sustaining lower rent values for property near the grounds and impropriety—such as whisky bottles found in the stalls and "being used as a resort for people whose moral sensibilities were anything but neute."

Throughout the 1880s, many of the tracks built across the country during the 1860s and 1870s were already waning and closing. There were sulky-specific racetracks already in Freeport, Dubuque and—most popularly—in Chicago. Rockford was tardy in creating a track site specifically for trotting horses but not in having a driving association. Dr. E.C. Dunn, Joseph W.

Hale and Frank G. Smith were the officers of a Rockford Driving Park Association in 1885. It is not completely evident whether this association was the same one created by Brown in 1868 or a different one, but it signifies that horse racing was still important to wealthy businessmen in Rockford throughout the late 1800s. The association bitterly complained about how the fairgrounds track was too small for good racing and proposed that the track be made into a half-mile track. If the track could not or would not be enlarged, the association threatened to build its own track. By 1889, the threats from the Rockford Driving Park Association became reality. Businessmen Frank Barnes, Bine Sturtevant, George Keyt, Dr. B.B. Page, H.H. Palmer, Let Halsted and C.C. Jones helped push the association to build a separate driving park for sulky horse racing in Rockford. In late October 1889, the Rockford Driving Park was incorporated, and subscriptions (investments) for the Driving Park Association were first collected. By mid-December, the association had collected $12,000 to purchase land but was not sure where the park would be officially located. The location of the park was assumed to be on the west side of Rockford, but the exact site was not determined for a month after the association was established. By December 27, the *Morning Star* reported:

> *While it is entirely certain that the Driving Club will be established, considerable hard hustling is still required to obtain the $25,000 required* [to build the track]. *Bine Sturtevant took the subscription paper Christmas day and before nightfall had collared $3,000, and yesterday Let Halsted succeeded in raising $650. This makes $20,650 already subscribed, and with extra exertions the balance can be cornered by Saturday, when the option on the Carney and Rice farms expires.*

On December 28, the Rockford Driving Park Association held its first meeting of investors. It had raised $24,000 as of that night, which was when the location for the park was to be decided. The investors were divided in two camps; half were in favor of buying the Dan Carney farm, and half were in favor of buying the Rice farm. Both farms were located in northwest Rockford, which was booming with development in housing since Rockford's population had doubled from 13,120 in 1880 to 23,584 in 1890. After Frank Smith called the meeting to order and informed the investors that the Winnebago Agricultural Society was in favor of the Carney site and could rent it from the association for $600 for its annual fair, the investors agreed on the Carney purchase.

Dan Carney came to Illinois from New York in 1845. He was employed by Frink and Walker as a stagecoach driver. In 1848, Carney made Rockford his permanent home. His farm was located on the northeast corner of Auburn Street and Rockton Avenue. Throughout the 1870s and until his death, Dan trained horses for sulky racing and had a mile-long track on his own farm, which was convenient for the association's needs.

In January 1890, a Chicago real estate developer offered Carney $18,000 for sixty acres east of his farmstead. The offer was declined. The *Daily Register* reported that "H.H. Palmer, acting as trustee for the driving park club, had recorded in the circuit clerk's office the agreement signed by Dan Carney, by which they claim that they bought his farm for a driving park. It is hinted…that Carney will be sued if he does not live up to his agreement." To the surprise of the Rockford Driving Park Association, the Carney farm was instead sold to city attorney Edward H. Marsh (backed by H.W. Price, Myron Bruner and Charlie Fox) for around $16,000 (after placing $5,600 down). The *Morning Star* reported on January 10: "It is expected that Mr. Price's intention is to run the streetcar line way out, erect houses along the line for rental, make the streetcar line help his property and the property help the line—in short, to build up a Pullman town to the north of Rockford and all things tend to prove the correctness of the theory." Marsh continued to buy land around what is now Huffman Boulevard, and the subdivision that grew became known as E.H. Marsh's Park View Subdivision. Carney stated that he knew nothing about the driving park "matter" and that the driving park club had not "produced" any money toward him for the sale of his property. The Rockford Driving Park Association members were furious. They stated that Carney should be barred from the track once it was built. The search began anew with alternative sites, which included acres around the Buckbee Greenhouses or William Lathrop's farm on the east side of Rockford. These sites were quickly dismissed as undesirable locations.

The Rockford Driving Park Association met at the opera house (operated by C.C. Jones) on January 14, 1890. During this meeting, members decided to locate the racetrack close to the original Carney tract. On January 16, the *Daily Gazette* announced that the "Driving Club" bought Sylvester B. Wilkins's farm for $9,000. Wilkins's farm was bordered by Overdene Avenue, Huffman Boulevard, the railroad tracks to the south and four lots west of Ridge Avenue. According to a brief statement in the *Daily Register* on July 12, 1890, Dan Carney liked the new driving park location, and the editor sarcastically added that Carney's feeling was natural. The Rockford Driving Park Association also bought a ten-acre strip of land along what is now Fulton Avenue in order to extend the property to Main Street. Despite these purchases, the final location for the driving park was in question.

In February, two aldermen offered the Rockford Driving Park Association bonuses of $1,500 to relocate the driving park to the south side of Rockford. They believed it would be easier for their working-class constituents to attend the races if the park were located on the south side. These offers were declined. On February 13, the *Daily Register* reported that the Rockford Driving Park Association directors drove to the Wilkins site to thoroughly inspect the land they had bought. There were no buildings on the property, corn stood on five acres of the land and there was a huge pile of straw (which they decided they could potentially use for opening day). They concluded that the Wilkins land was actually better than the Carney tract because it was a little sandier, which meant that it could dry out faster after rains and allow for more racing or training to be conducted.

To get to the park, the streetcar ran from Auburn Street north on Huffman Boulevard and stopped to drop off passengers at the main gate. It then continued east on Fulton Avenue and on to North Main Street. Streetcars had just been developed and were considered a new mode of transportation in the United States at the time. Throughout the month of April 1890, there were a number of discussions as to where and how the streetcar would be funded in the booming North End. A deal was made between several parties (the real estate developer H.W. Price, realtor W.F. Huffman and the Rockford Driving Park Association) in which they divided the $15,000 cost of the extension. The streetcar ran down the middle of the street, and horses, carriages and pedestrians traveled on the sides.

A small problem developed with the streetcar company during opening week. Workers worked on the electric car lines to the park until the last minute. Despite their best efforts, the electric wires were four blocks short of the park entrance. There was supposed to be a shipment of new electric cars, but they did not arrive until the week after the park opened. Subsequently, the streetcar company ran all three of the electric cars with two trailers it did have on the "Driving Park Circuit." The rest of the city was serviced by horse-drawn cars. The streetcar company fixed this problem by providing horse cars from the wire's end to the front gate. Today, Huffman Boulevard ceases to be a true boulevard at Fulton Avenue because that's where the gate to the driving park was located. The St. Paul and Milwaukee Railroad was supposed to build a small depot near the main entrance, but the depot was also not constructed by the proposed opening day of August 26, 1890.

The association originally planned for the track to be built in a "pear shape," because J.P. Sauber (who owned the land west of the park) refused to sell any of his land to the association, and the railroad was located at the southern end of the park. Other reasons behind the unique shape of the original proposed tracks were that the spectators could clearly see the race, and the straightaways would allow for faster track times. By April 12, 1890, the association had decided against the pear shape and agreed on a traditional oval. The traditional oval-shaped track was a good long-term decision, because automobiles and motorcycles could not have made the "hairpin" turn.

The grandstand was located on the west side of the track and was modeled after the grandstand in Chicago's Washington Park. Spectators were comfortable because the stands could seat two thousand people, and there were one thousand easy, opera-styled chairs for ladies. However, after spectators entered through the southeastern gates (near where Fulton Avenue runs into Huffman Boulevard), they had to walk a quarter-mile along the south side of the track just to get to the grandstand. The *Morning Star* complained as it proposed that a streetcar line or railway spur be laid to directly transport spectators to the grandstand seats. This proposal was never acted upon, possibly due to the location of the stalls and not wanting to commingle incoming horses and spectators waiting at the gate. The location of the grandstand was chosen to keep the sun out of spectators' eyes and provide a great view of the homestretch, but the long walk irritated many spectators instead. The association's directors believed that the entrance could be moved later to the southwest side of the park, yet this modification was never made. Underneath the grandstand (out of sight and earshot) were "pool seller stands" for betting. In front of the grandstand was an area for reporters. On the other side of the track, in front of the grandstand, was the octagonal, parasol-covered judge's stand. Horses and drivers entered the track from the 150 horse stalls on the west side of the track and south of the grandstand. Spectators got "good looks" at the horses and drivers before they bet on them.

Construction of the park began on April 23 and was to be completed by August 26. Throughout the construction process, approximately two hundred men worked on putting the stalls, fences, water pipe, judge's stand, track and other details together. The lumber was easily brought in by the railroad. By May 23, the track was dredged and ready for racing. Fresh water was available for the horses and the spectators through the one thousand feet of water pipes. A windmill was built just south of the grandstand to provide pressure for the

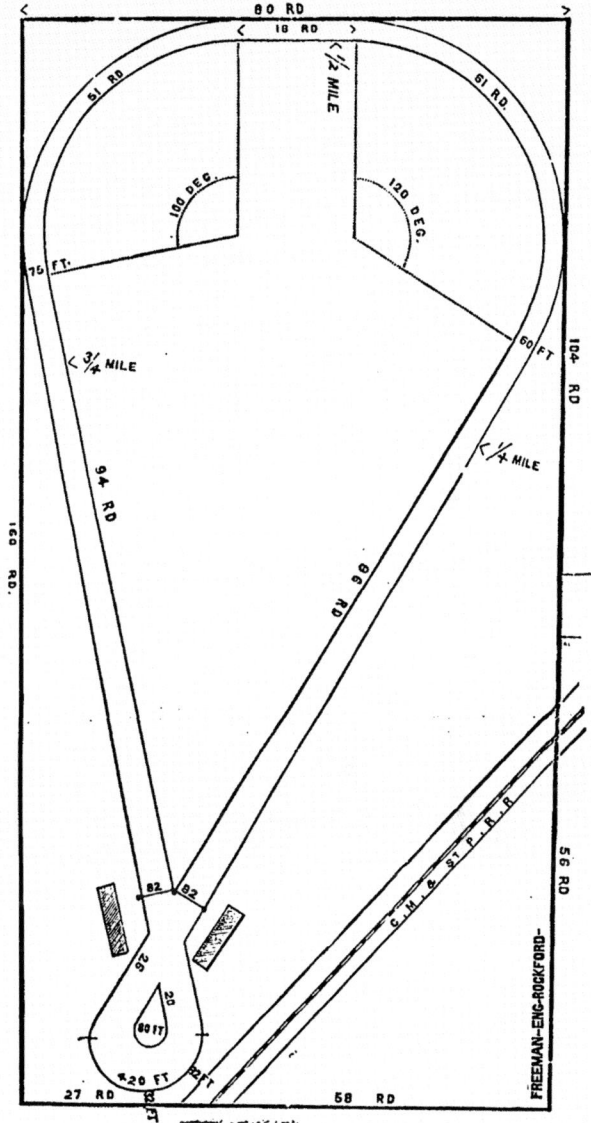

The "pear-shaped" track design was originally purposed to increase straightaways and speed. *From "A Two Minute Track,"* Morning Star, *March 27, 1890.*

system. A state-of-the-art "sprinkling" wagon was also purchased to water down the track in case of intolerable dust. By the end of July, there were over twenty horses stabled and practicing on the track (by mid-August, that number had doubled), and the grandstand was in the process of being built. There was no hesitation. There were just a few association meetings, and, suddenly, a complete racetrack had formed in an open field in a few months.

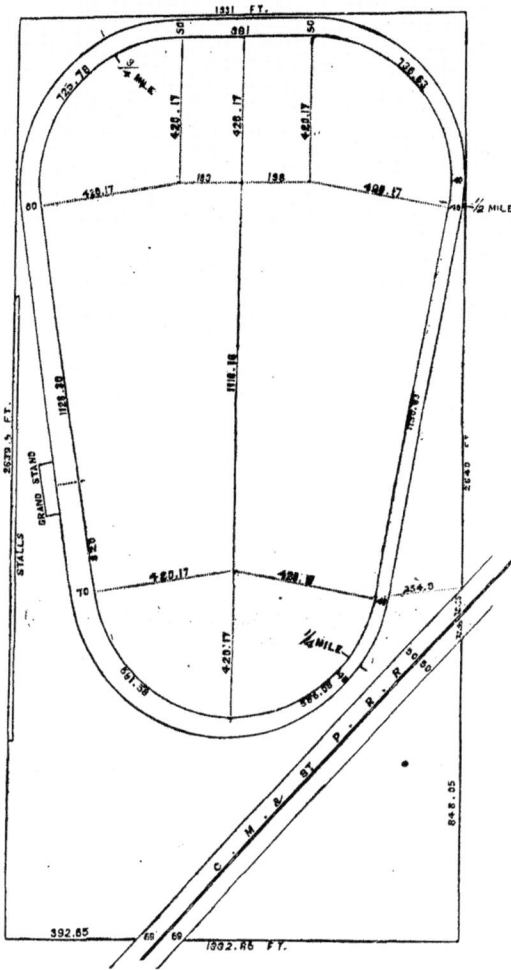

The finalized track layout.
From Morning Star, *February 1, 1891.*

On August 2, it was reported that H.H. Palmer (the designer of the track) spent all day and possibly the night at the track, making sure that timely progress was made on the track. It was thought that the famous horse Hambletonian would be registered for races, but his stardom must have been too great for him to come to Rockford. Two horse-owners could not wait for opening day and raced their horses for twenty-five dollars on August 7. Doe Walsh's Sailor Girl raced against B.C. Kimlin's Cherry Picker. Sailor Girl won the race, but Walsh was nice enough to give Kimlin back the twenty-five-dollar bet. By August 17, the *Morning Star*, worried for the sanity of the driving park directors, reported:

> If somebody, anybody, everybody don't take hold of Cassius Columbus Jones, Frank Gustavus Smith, Lester Brunswick Halsted, George Melanchton Keyt, Benjamin Franklin Barnes, Thomas Diametricus Reber, Hoar Hound Palmer, Bartonnis Baredo Page, Zebulon Biology Sturtevant, they will go crazy. Of course, this doesn't mean that they will lose their mental balance, but it does suggest that their friends must look after them. Every day, every hour, every minute, and for the matter of time—every second they can be seen on the street corners talking hoss.

The dates August 26 through 29, 1890, were selected for the park's official grand opening. August 28 was selected as "ladies' day," and it was suggested that the ladies receive a picture of the driving park for attending the races. The *Morning Star* believed that factories should close and a holiday should be declared so that everyone in Rockford could witness the races. The purses for the races averaged between $600 and $800, and there were two races each day, with ten- to fifteen-horse fields. Horses came from across Northern Illinois and from Wisconsin, Ohio, Michigan and Kentucky. Hotels filled up. The Chicago, Milwaukee and St. Paul Railway offered round-trip tickets for fifteen cents from downtown (the train stopped at State Street) so people could come to the track. The Dubuque Trotting Association president and the Stephenson County Fair superintendent came to see the action and size up the horses. General admission was fifty cents, and it was an extra twenty-five cents to be in the grandstand. Seats along the quarter stretch were also an extra twenty-five cents. Spectator carriages were parked inside the "paddock" or in the infield of the track for one dollar. The Rockford Watch Company Band played tunes between the heats of races. Spectators could buy pretzels from Frank Schmauss and cigars from another vendor. There was also a driving park dining hall that could seat up to five hundred people.

Approximately two thousand people attended the first day of races on August 26. There was a sixty-dollar fee to enter a horse into a race. Race winners had to win the majority of a race's heats. For example, the first race on the first day had four heats. The first heat had thirteen horses. A horse named Irene won all of the first race's heats except the third. The averages of the heat times determined a race's winning order. Therefore, Irene's owners claimed a race purse of $300, second place won $150, third place won $90 and fourth place won $60. Yet things were not always clearly won.

The *Daily Register* cried foul about the first race winner because the winner outclassed its competitors since the horse led throughout by wide margins, which made the races unexciting. The second race's heats were postponed (due to rain) until the second day. Two drivers were fined five dollars for crowding the pole or interference during the heats. Harry Kelly was the only horse owned and trained in Winnebago County that raced on the first day. The *Daily Register* commented that he "might as well have stayed in the stable" due to his poor finishes.

The second day of racing, August 27, had clear weather and more controversy. Red Flame, a race winner, was unique, because during the previous year, the horse pulled a butcher's cart. It was believed that the driver held the horse back in order to not win the first two heats so as to split the prize money with another driver. After the second heat, Red Flame's driver was advised to let the horse go, and it easily won the remaining heats.

The third day of racing was "ladies' day." The attendance for that day averaged around four to six thousand spectators. During the second heat of race number five, two of the driver's carriages collided, which made for some excitement, but the horse, Prize, won all of the race's heats and took first place. A horse named Nobby was favored to win in the next race by most of the ladies in attendance and easily won all of the heats except one. Despite his prospects of winning, in the second heat, Nobby's driver was found guilty of interference and was placed last despite crossing the line first. Since the day's races concluded fairly quickly and the crowd was still rather large, the association decided to run an additional consolation race that day.

The last day of racing was Saturday, August 30. In the third heat of the first race, B.B. and El Monarch crossed the wire at the same time, but it did not matter, because B.B. had won all of the other heats. Fred Arthur was challenged to beat his best time of 2:12. He failed in front of a crowd of six thousand people. The association decided to end the day with another consolation race.

If Rockford spectators had not taken in the day of races, the Barnum & Bailey Circus was in town to entertain as well. Members of the Rockford Driving Park Association netted $2,500 in profits. A few weeks later, the Winnebago County Agricultural Society had its exhibition. The agricultural society decided to repair the grounds and hold horse and sulky races on its own grounds and not at the driving park. The Rockford newspapers continued to print editorials begging the agricultural society to reconsider, but to no avail. The fairgrounds track was only a third of a mile long instead of a mile, like the track at Rockford Driving Park. Many of the horses that had run at the driving park during its opening days remained in Rockford to run in the agricultural society's races. Perhaps if the fair had been held there, the park would have been far more remembered and had a completely different history.

Throughout the months following the August opening, there were few mentions of activity at the driving park in Rockford newspapers. Freeman's Livery Stables mentioned the driving park in its advertisements for carriages. It was suggested that the driving park join the racing circuit between Dubuque and Independence, but the association declined the offer because the directors believed that they had made a big enough profit from the August races. This decision may have hurt the park's future, because as a member of a racing circuit, the park could have held regular races and gained wider attention. Instead, improvements were made, and a few races were held between locally owned horses to settle bets until general races were conducted in June and August 1891. However, the driving park had competition for spectators on the northwest side that year, because Harlem Amusement Park and a baseball park had opened to the public. As early as July 9, 1892, the *Morning Star* reported that the Rockford Driving Park Association would no longer hold race meets due to low attendance numbers. The writer complained that Rockford was too small to support a racetrack and citizens were "too Puritan" for racing. In fact, racing and gambling were not as widely accepted as a trend in the North as they were in the South due to northern America's "Puritan" heritage. Racing horses involved betting and drinking liquor (which was not allowed in the park but was sold anyway), which were not family-oriented activities. In fact, liquor was a hotly debated issue in Rockford during the turn of the century. Despite this report, the story of the Rockford Driving Park did not end in 1892. It was just the beginning of almost fifty years of triumphs and tragedies.

2.

EXCITEMENT ON AND OFF
THE TRACK

The opening days of the Rockford Driving Park in August 1890 brought a $2,500 to $3,500 profit for the Rockford Driving Park Association. Secretary C.C. Jones reconsidered a deal in which Rockford would be part of a racing circuit including other parks located in Elgin, Janesville, Freeport and Aurora. Three "meetings," or racing events, were planned for 1891, with the first meet to be held in June. The future of the driving park looked bright, but accidents and incidents seemed to forecast its future.

Trainers brought their horses to the stables as soon as the track was ready for them that spring. In April, a trainer named Matthew Maloney from Belvidere was exercising a "green" horse named Babe when one of the horse's rear legs got caught in one of its foreleg hobbles. The horse toppled headfirst, and the force of the impact threw Maloney over the horse's head. The horse was uninjured, but Maloney's leg was broken in three places. On May 4, another trainer was exercising his horse when that horse stumbled and fell. The trainer was also thrown over the horse's head, but he was not injured and managed to quickly gain control of the horse's reins and hold the animal until help arrived.

Another meet was held from June 10 to June 13, 1891. The first day of races was not promising. Spectators could not ride on the Van Arsdale–, Huffman- or Spaulding-sponsored "Tally-Ho" wagon to the track, because profits from the wagon's service to the park did not make enough for its owners during the track's 1890 opening days. Storm clouds floated over the park in the afternoon, which kept spectators away. The races were reported to be slow, and most of the favorites won. In addition, Harlem Park and the baseball park were open, and the circus performed in town at the same time. On the second day of racing, the grandstand had empty seats despite attendance amounting to three thousand spectators. The *Morning Star* bitterly complained that there were hardly any spectators from Freeport, Elgin or Janesville (the sister cities of the racing circuit). One of the streetcars that brought spectators to the track on Huffman Boulevard "spread" (became uncoupled) and left several cars on the track. Races were held until eight o'clock at night, and according to the *Daily Register Gazette*, events spilled over into additional days due to the large fields of horses and false starts. Races on the third day lasted so long that they spilled into the final day of racing. The grandstand for that day was "filled beautifully," but a large portion of them were "rank outsiders," according to the *Daily Register Gazette*. The *Daily Register Gazette* editor continued, "With 25,000 to draw from the percentage of Rockford people who attended the races was only infinitesimal. While the meeting was a splendid success, it was not as overwhelmingly successful as it would have been with better attendance of our people." Newspaper columnists first complained about not having enough people come from surrounding cities, then they complained when people did exactly that. The positive side for the association was that by the end of the second day, profits already exceeded those of the 1890 opening meet. The success opened new opportunities for the park.

The Rockford Cycling Club also held an enormous bicycle meet on July 4 in the park. There were over five hundred cyclists in attendance. Approximately ten thousand people attended the bicycle races, but twenty thousand people went to Harlem Park. Other purposes were found for the track as well, such as a footrace challenge between two men to be settled at the park. The more purposes the park could serve, the more people came and enjoyed it, which increased its overall vitality. However, in this early stage of the park's life, horse racing remained the main use for the grounds.

To increase the excitement for the next meeting in August, the association announced that it would offer a $9,000 total purse (though by late July, the total purse was reduced to $8,000). The purse was the largest ever to be offered in Northern Illinois. The total of horses training on the grounds rose to one hundred as word spread across the Midwest about the park.

The second Rockford Driving Park Association meeting of 1891 was held from August 11 through August 14. Secretary C.C. Jones negotiated a contract with the trotting dog Jo to trot along a trotting pony in tandem, and the owner of pacing horse Roy Wilkes was slated to try to beat his best time of 2:15 to add novelty to the racing days. The Rockford Watch Company Band performed, and vehicles could be parked on the park grounds for free. John Clarke and Jonathan Peacock were to sell soft drinks only (there were numerous beer stands in the Freeport Driving Park, but none legally in Rockford's). Herb Lewis sold cigars, an African American woman sold ice cream, George Wilde handled the betting pools and Colonel Becker from Aurora was in charge of the betting wheel game. There were 137 horses from across the Midwest—as far south as Arkansas and as far north as Michigan—registered to race over the four days despite higher, 10 percent race purse entry fees (the high fee was likely due to the Rockford park just being built, because most other parks only charged 5 percent). This increase in entry fees also may have been to cover the cost of the purse. Rockford's drivers and horses included B.C. Kimlin's trotter Tommy Root and William Clark's Hillberry. Matthew Maloney recovered from his April crash and drove many horses. The newspapers speculated for days leading up to the event about which horses would win and whether the nationally recognized horse named Nelson would come to Rockford; he did not. As horsemen and spectators poured into Rockford, they filled the hotels, patronized the blacksmith shops, bought newspapers and ate at the restaurants. The area's economy benefited heartily from race days.

The recent rains and new track graders made the track conditions perfect for the four-day meet. Spectators could not predict race winners, which led to exciting races. Race judge Walker was tested because the heats had contenders trotting and pacing, as if they were pairs, toward the finish line. There was no flash photography to determine race winners. In one of the heats of the first race, eight horses ran side-by-side for a time. The attendance on the first day was around one thousand people, which was low compared to previous opening days, but numbers increased as the meet continued.

Not all of the drivers found success. The horse Pat Downing stumbled and fell. His driver, George Eggleton, was thrown off his seat but managed to maintain control of the horse until others came to help him. The horse was led back to the stables unharmed, and Eggleton was fined ten dollars for driving in front of the pole horse numerous times. An African American driver drove Abullah McGregor. The horse came in last out of four because his driver claimed that he was "racing for fun."

On the last day of races, four thousand people came to witness them. Despite the attendance numbers, the association lost $1,500, because entry fees and ticket sales did not make up for the purse costs. The August driving park meet seemed to come to a quiet end inside of the park, but the same could not be said outside.

Alexander "Cinch" Moulton was an African American stableman who worked at the driving park. He made a bet with a Chicago horse doctor named C.H. Foster. When Foster lost his bet, he did not pay. Moulton caught up with Foster in the lobby of the Holland House. An altercation broke out, and Foster kicked and held Moulton. When Foster potentially produced a gun, Moulton managed to escape his hold and threw Foster to the floor. The police arrived on the scene and took both men to jail. Moulton and Foster were brought before a judge and fined ten dollars each.

Another off-track drama unfolded between the Rockford Driving Park Association and the Winnebago Agricultural Society. Gambling and horse racing were considered "sinful" in the United States as far back as the 1600s. States such as New York, which was a leader in harness racing, legally prohibited gambling on horse racing in the early 1800s. Rockford faced the issue, too. Asa E. Cutler was the president of the agricultural society for a year. He disliked the gambling and drinking that occurred at the driving park. He, along with J.H. King, approached Rockford Driving Park Association secretary Jones about the "immoral activities." Jones told Cutler and King that the betting wheel generated revenue for the association and that he would do nothing in response. Cutler was not satisfied. A warrant for the arrest of Colonel Becker—for illegal gambling—was served, and the wheel officially stopped spinning.

Lawrence McDonald accused Cutler of trying to destroy the society's annual fair. It was believed that the Rockford Driving Park Association scheduled its September meet at the same time as the society's annual fair out of revenge for Cutler's actions against the wheel. In the Second National Bank, McDonald loudly announced to all of the patrons within that "Cutler is trying to kill the fair…with his narrow ideas. He's been acting president [of the society] one year and has done more to hurt the prospects of the society than anyone else. We ought to vote him out of the presidency without giving him a chance to resign." Cutler denied the accusation and stated that he acted on behalf of concerned citizens. The agricultural society held sulky/harness races, too, so the fair's fields of pacers and trotters would be reduced along with the crowds. Debate continued about whether the society should continue to host the fair on the fairgrounds or at the driving park. Matthew Hardy believed that the fairgrounds should be converted into a public park in order to provide the city some "breathing room." The wheel and alcohol activities and accusations did not go away in the months that followed.

Reverend W.A. Phillips, of Court Street Methodist Episcopal Church, took notice of the activities at the driving park, too. During the late 1800s, a national religious movement called the Social Gospel Movement developed. Washington Gladden, a leader of the national movement, believed that industrialization had created many of the social ills of the United States. Gambling, alcohol abuse, prostitution and other ills were caused by poverty due to low wages. The movement's main objective was to guide people to salvation by emulating the life of Jesus and by putting aside earthly desires and helping people through good works. In a sermon entitled, "The Driving Park and the Wheel of Fortune or Shall Rockford Be Bulldozed by Gamblers?," Phillips preached, "The city has now reached a condition when it must be determined whether it shall retain the moral status that has belonged to it in the past or be handed over to the gamblers to do as they please." The religious community continued to attack the park. Harlem Park had no such religious qualms. In fact, many religious services were held at Harlem Park during Chautauqua events.

The September meeting promised not only racing but also sideshows (like the Freeport Driving Association's meeting, which was held at the beginning of August 1891). Coinciding with the September meet was the agricultural society fair, the opening of an opera house and Labor Day activities. Special detectives were hired for the September meet to prevent cheating between drivers and the betting boxes. The day's specialties were announced in the *Morning Star*. Tuesday was "ladies' day" (they were admitted free of charge), and the association agreed to run its first jockey-horse running race, the "Rockford Derby." On Thursday, special trains ran to the park, and Nelson, the nationally recognized horse from Maine, was to break his previous speed record. Someone placed a fifty-dollar bet that he would succeed.

The grocery store owners in town closed their doors to allow their workers a chance to go to the fair or races. The Germania Society also changed its meeting date, and the area schools were closed for the fair. Excuses for not going to the races ran slim. On Tuesday, September 1, trotting and running races were held. There were two Rockford horses entered in the trotting races. Independence was driven by Thomas Reber, and Ferd Keyt was driven by Matthew Maloney. No Rockford horses were run in the eight-horse field running race, but the crowd full of ladies cheered loudly during its two heats. A jockey fell from his horse in front of the grandstand during one of the heats, but, thankfully, he was uninjured. The trotting race was next, which garnered much excitement. The *Morning Star* reported: "It was in this [fifth] heat that [C.H.] Nelson, who was driving Brownie, came to grief over on the back stretch. He fell off from the sulky, upsetting the latter and starting his horse on a dead run for home, with the broken shaft on his back [the sulky was upside down as the horse ran free]. But the race went on; the runaway horse passing the trotters at the last quarter and got out of their way before they reached the wire." Brownie's driver got to his feet and limped across the track. The horse was captured and stayed unharmed in the barn for the rest of the meet. As if that were not enough excitement, in the sixth heat, the driver of Townsend Chief, S.L. Canton, cut off the driver of Hendricks so quickly that Hendricks almost came to a standstill. The crowd called foul, and the decision of the sixth heat was held over until the next day. The *Daily Register Gazette* reported that there were around three thousand people in attendance for "ladies' day," or "Blue Ribbon Day," as it was also called.

By the third day, ten to twenty thousand spectators came to see Nelson's national trotting record fall. Carriages and people lined all of the fences. Trotting and pacing races were run first. Then, the starter called for Nelson. He trotted along the track with a runner-horse stablemate at great speed, then Judge Walker rang the bell at the wire for silence as they checked their stopwatches. The wind was against Nelson, and the runner horse outran him in the last quarter-stretch, which made the horse slow down instead of keeping his speed. His time was still impressive (2:12), but it was not enough to break his nationally held speed record of 2:10. The last race of the day was a running race. Excitement in this race came not from the horses or jockeys, but from a card seller. The *Morning Star* reported on the event:

> *The runners were just finishing up when Frank Bauch, one of Phillips's scorecard sellers, started across the track. He supposed that all the horses had passed the wire and jumped from the fence. Just as he did so, Hyprun, one of the runners that was trailing, struck him like a cannonball and knocked him against the fence. The horse flew by, and the man lay apparently dead on the track.*

People began to crowd onto the track. Two doctors tended to Bauch, then he was transported to the hospital, where he received stitches to his lip and above his eyebrows. On the fourth and final day, Nelson was expected to run one more time to become known as the fastest trotter in the nation, but his leg was swollen in the morning, and his owner refused to risk his horse's health. The attendance numbers were lower than on Thursday, and the races were typical. According to the *Morning Star*, $20,000 passed through the pool boxes, $2,600 was made from ticket sales and one thousand carriages were parked in the infield. Despite all of the activities, races and Nelson's record-breaking attempts, the association cleared only $700 in profit. The businesses of Rockford, however, made substantial profits from all of the events, since people stayed in hotels, ate in restaurants and used the public transportation system.

The September meet once again ended with drama outside the park. John "Jack" Mahon was removed from the park during the races for his disorderly conduct. When the races concluded, he waited for policeman J.B. Rowan (presumably, the officer who removed him). Mahon possessed some rocks and targeted Rowan. Mahon was arrested and charged with attempted murder. Mahon requested a "change of venue" from Judge Craig to Judge Weld. He was fined $100 plus court costs, which would be dropped if he had good behavior while serving his sixty-day prison sentence.

William Hurley was a jockey at the driving park. His boss was displeased with him, believing that Hurley mismanaged his mount. Hurley got into a verbal argument with his boss and was fired. He then went to the agricultural fair to "drown his sorrows" and possibly pick up another job. When a fair official refused to let him in (probably because he lacked the money for entry), Hurley threw a rock at him. He was arrested and fined four dollars for disorderly conduct. Since he lacked the money to pay, he spent some nights in jail before returning to his native Tennessee.

More off-track drama developed in September. According to the *Rockford Morning Star*, *Freeport Democrat* newspapermen named James Cowley, George Sheetz and Frank Bering stated that the crowd located in the quarter-stretch of the driving park during the last race meet "was about the toughest aggregation of humanity that they ever saw anywhere." Sheetz, the editor of the Freeport paper, denied the accusation, and the *Rockford Morning Star* claimed that the people who crowded that area were not from Rockford. Accusations of "tough" or ungentlemanly men or conduct may have hurt the park's reputation as a place for respectable entertainment. Ladies, and especially families, would likely not have wanted to be near this type of crowd.

Not only did the park gain an ungentlemanly reputation, it also could not keep up with its debts. Orson Truman built a barn on the driving park grounds for Louis B. Bronson for $686 after Bronson's barn caught fire earlier in the year. Bronson paid Truman $300, then sold the barn to Charles H. Faulkner and the Rockford Driving Park Association. Truman went through the circuit court and obtained a mechanics lien against the association, Faulkner and Bronson to get the remaining $386 owed to him. Was the debt due to Faulkner and Bronson's lack of funds, or was the association in monetary trouble? This may have stifled future investment in the park.

The negative publicity continued. On October 2, Reverend Phillips of the Court Street Methodist Church announced that he would leave the church. However, his messages/sermons against gambling and illegal liquor sales at the driving park resonated. A small group of Rockford citizens demanded that a grand jury be formed and the state's attorney prosecute officials who allowed the illegal activities. The suit brought against Becker's "wheel of fortune" men by the State of Illinois was dropped in circuit court, but the association was not going to get off as easily.

A grand jury quickly formed and called several high-ranking officers of the association to provide testimony. H.W. Price was called three times in one day. Constable Amasa Hutchins testified that he broke up the "wheelmen" and arrested them but left soon afterward and did not see any other violations. Charley Whipple was next. He testified that he, along with Cutler and King, went to Secretary Jones to shut down the wheel. Jones told them that the wheel made too much money to shut it down. Whipple also testified that a bar was operated by John Clarke and six assistants. Apparently, Clarke sold more than just soft drinks (as he originally advertised). When the sheriff's men arrested the "wheelmen," the bar was closed. After the sheriff's men left, the bar reopened and served beer to many men, including Mott Utter, A.W. Fay, F.V. Perry, P.L. Sullivan (a Rockford police officer), C. Calkins, H.W. Price, W.O. Wormwood and T. Derwent. Whipple's was the last testimony recorded on day one of the grand jury. Price was called for a fourth time and appeared on day two. Despite a day and a half of testimony, the jury found all those subpoenaed to be innocent. A twist in the case occurred when the *Morning Star* reported some of the trial information. The jury foreman, Mr. Treat, was sentenced to sixty days in jail for slipping information to reporters. Clarke pleaded guilty on three counts of illegal liquor-selling at the park and was fined a total of $322.30. The lawsuits, religious sermons and violence certainly did not help the park's reputation. Rockford's population did not completely support the park; meanwhile, Harlem Park had a reputation for being completely family-oriented. Most historians also would not want to recognize the negative failures of the driving park in their works.

On a positive note, it was announced on October 2, 1891, that local bicyclists considered another race meet to be held at the park within the same month. However, the driving park's future was foggy. The first hint of the park's potential end was published in the *Morning Star* on October 24, 1891. It stated that "the base ballists [baseball players] should lease the driving park as it is possible that the racing business is ended." Some wanted the park to be annexed by the city. Others believed that the park was still a place for racing, because Matthew Maloney brought more horses into his stables for training at the park.

A new driving park board of directors met in February 1892. Thomas Reber and Bine Sturtevant became president and vice president, respectively. Secretary Jones was replaced by James McKee. The committee quickly decided to hold another horse-racing meet over the July 4 holiday week, and the purse total was an unheard-of $20,000 in prize money. Money talks, the paper reported, but by March, cooler heads must have prevailed, and the purse total was lowered considerably—to $5,900. To create a more family-friendly atmosphere, W.B. Reynolds's Circus was to also perform on the grounds along with Madam Maranette's show featuring ten trained horses. On April 15, the board of directors met and decided to begin organizing a second meet for September 13–16. The projected purse total was $16,000. The news kept getting better when the *Daily Register Gazette* reported that an eastern horseman wanted to build a $10,000 barn to train his horses on the driving park grounds. On June 20, President Reber and Secretary McKee secured mortgages from Emily Graham (the wife of Julius Graham) and Clara Hill to financially sustain the park and its activities. However, people continued to write editorials against the park for its immoral gambling practices and alcohol consumption.

Throughout May and June 1892, rain created floods throughout Rockford. The association took the weather outlook into account and reduced the schedule for the July meet to only July 4. No other driving parks in the area held any races before Rockford's. On that day, the weather was perfect, and five thousand people attended. The race results were not recorded in local newspapers, and instead, more column space was given to Harlem Park activities. The *Morning Star* complained that the driving park should have displayed more patriotism than just horse racing and Madam Maranette's trained-horse show. The *Morning Star* also blamed the "Puritans" and "do-gooders" of Rockford for the Rockford Driving Park Association's low receipts and misery. No liquor was officially sold at the driving park, but people believed that spectators brought their own. Profits from liquor and gambling were lost due to moralists. Rockford also did not have a large enough leisure class to support the driving park, because the majority of the city's population was working class. Nor could the driving park entice enough people to travel to Rockford to make up for the lack of the city's support. The July 4 one-day meet did not provide a big profit, and the association incurred a $1,000 debt. The cancelation of the September meet was announced on July 9. Soon after, the Freeport Driving Park closed for a time due to a lack of profits, despite allowing gambling. The Des Moines, Iowa track also closed on August 20. It seemed like Rockford was not the only track facing financial ruin.

Survival meant that the park had to serve other purposes. The *Spectator* reported several events that occurred there. African Americans celebrated Emancipation Day on August 1, a local cyclist beat his best mile time and the Rockford Gun Club held a shooting contest. These other events gave the park new life while other parks around the nation were beginning to disappear.

Rumors flew throughout the month of August. The park was supposedly sold to a Mr. McCollough. Harry H. Carney, from Iowa, came to Rockford to propose a deal on behalf of a Mr. Bride from Chicago. Bride supposedly planned to lease the driving park for legally clean horse racing. F. Barton from Independence, Iowa, or Bert Cobb from Darlington, Wisconsin, were also reported as wanting to lease the park from the association. The Winnebago Agricultural Society was rumored to have offered to buy the park if the price was right. Throughout all of these rumors, horses continued to be trained, but many left for other tracks. No signs of future racing were apparent, and the park became deserted by the end of August.

On September 3, Secretary McKee announced future directors' meetings in early November to discuss the sale and future of the driving park and to elect officers for the association on November 29. Yet again, all of the previous board members resigned, and another new board was elected. Ed Lathrop was elected president, C.F. Henry was elected vice president and the secretary position remained vacant. Since the board had just been installed, it was too late to organize a meeting for the spring season. The board advised the public that the races held in 1893 would be on the "highest moral plane." Alcohol and gambling were prohibited, and they debated selling cigars. The months of February and March 1893 flew by, and still the association made no announcement about a meeting to be held. It seemed that the new association was lacking motivation and activity due to a lack of local interest. The national financial panic of 1893 also did not help matters. Most of the Rockford Driving Park Association members were businessmen; their first priorities involved protecting their own business ventures instead of the park. During times of economic depression, many people seek entertainment to escape their woes. Harlem Park was able to survive because it was consistently open and reliably offered family-friendly entertainment, which the driving park could not do.

3

FAILED DREAMS

*T*he *Morning Star* railed against the new Rockford Driving Park Association board and angrily demanded, "Wake up gentlemen. Give us a week of racing and, if it doesn't pay, rent the park for farm purposes and no more will the matter be agitated." The year was 1893, and it was the third season of the driving park. As the nation faced an economic crisis, the park that was once considered the fastest and best track in the country struggled to remain in existence. Ironically, a former foe of the association came to the park's rescue.

Harry Carney (son of Dan Carney, who had refused to sell his land to the association) could not wait for the association to take action. In early April, he proposed to area businessmen that they sponsor races, thus generating money for purses. Finally, on May 25, the association held a meeting and decided that races would be held from June 21 through June 24. As a reward for his efforts, Harry Carney was appointed to the vacant secretary position of the Rockford Driving Park Association. Carney secured money for a hotel, merchant and manufacturer purse. The *Morning Star* believed that high spectator attendance was possible because there were no other significant events scheduled for the summer.

Carney made an official public statement on June 5 and arranged headquarters at the Nelson Hotel. Full of energy, he took control of the organization so completely that one of the association's directors inquired about where the office of the association was now located. Carney continued the commitment to the prohibition of gambling and alcohol on the park grounds, and only good racing—with 75 to 125 horses—would be held. Carney also made the argument that attending the races on all four days was cheaper than attending the Chicago's World's Fair for one day. Nationally known horsemen, including Budd Doble, who invented the modern sulky, were supposed to be in attendance. Carney believed that farmers should attend the races because the Winnebago Agricultural Society was not holding a fair that year, and it would be their only chance to congregate. Carney almost pleaded with the public to come, stating that the park had fallen into $6,000 to $7,000 in debt over the previous two years, and if racing was to continue in Rockford, the public should support the park. Yet, it was not the public who clamored for the park; wealthy businessmen wanted it from the start.

As proposed, horses came from as far south as Texas and as far north as Minnesota. On the opening day of the races, June 20, ladies could attend for free, and the Fitzgerald Band was contracted to play between races. However, nature spoiled all hopes of racing. Rain poured just before the first horses were called by the starter. The band played, hoping that the rain would pass. It did not. The races were suspended.

"Two Days' Events Crowded into One" was the subtitle of a newspaper article covering day two. To advertise the event, Carney paid a military band to play on a streetcar throughout the city. Handbills were dispersed everywhere. Ladies were still allowed free admission (men paid fifty cents). The Rockford Watch Company closed at noon to allow its workers to attend the races (the *Morning Star* encouraged other businesses to follow suit). Carney contracted a bus operator to transport spectators from the gate to the grandstand so they would not have to walk so far.

Ominous rain clouds gathered, but the inclement weather held off. The track was solid and elastic—good for racing. Attendance peaked at 1,600. Apparently, not all of the races could be run in one day, so three races were completed on the following day. The favorites mostly won, but excitement was generated by the horse named Blonde, because the gelding paced the fastest heat in the nation, setting a record of 2:19. Carney arranged a "local roadsters" race at the end of the second day. The entries had to be Winnebago County horses with Winnebago County drivers. Apparently, the local men could not line up properly for the beginning of the race. Race judge Harry F. Loper rang the false start bell repetitively. Loper became so frustrated at the local drivers that he called the drivers to the judges' stand and threatened to fine drivers twenty-five dollars if they passed the pole horse. Three heats were run, but the race remained unfinished, and it was postponed to a third day of racing. One day of racing had quickly become many with thousands in attendance.

Despite all of Harry Carney's efforts, the association's meet was unprofitable. The *Morning Star* commented: "It is worthy of note that the gentlemen who have been clamoring for a racetrack with moral appendages did not take time to attend the meeting." An enterprise that does not make money normally does not stay in business long, nor is it remembered. Nonetheless, Carney chartered the *Arrow* boat for all of the drivers, owners and other VIPs in appreciation of their efforts. Perhaps by doing so, he was attempting to create future business for the park. Carney believed that an autumn meeting would be profitable because there were no Winnebago County Agricultural Society races at that time to compete with theirs, and the park did not remain idle for long.

The first "ordinary," or high-wheel, bicycles were developed in the 1860s. These bicycles had a large front wheel because they were not powered by a gear and chain. This style of bicycle was difficult to mount and maintain balance upon, and collisions with pedestrians were not uncommon. In the 1880s, new "safety" bicycles gained popularity because the wheels were smaller, equally sized and pneumatic. By the 1890s, a great bicycle craze swept the nation. Manufacturing companies and sales and service shops opened. Velodromes (circular-banked wooden bicycle tracks) and smoother roads were built to accommodate them. Bicycle clubs formed nationwide. Everyday citizens used them to gain greater independence, especially women. Fashion changed as feminine bustles (a type of hoop and skirt) fell out of favor, and bloomers (shortened cotton ankle-length pants worn underneath skirts) became fashionable. Susan B. Anthony was impressed by the bicycle, stating, "Let me tell you what I think of bicycling. I think it has done more to emancipate women than anything else in the world. I stand and rejoice every time I see a woman ride by on a wheel. It gives woman a feeling of freedom and self-reliance." Bicycles were cheaper to maintain than horses and could be ridden anywhere. Rockford had its fair share of bicycle riders.

On July 4, the park hosted the Rockford Bicycle Club's "Cycle Tournament." Local businessmen supported the tournament with cigar boxes and silk umbrellas, a life-insurance policy and a diamond ring as prizes. Prizes were displayed in the windows of C.F. Henry and Company. Three hundred cyclists from Elgin, along with members from every Chicago bicycle club, attended. F.J. Osmond, the English Champion rider, was also in attendance. The Mendelssohn and St. Cecelia Clubs women's groups announced that their members were to attend. This meant that Rockford women were actively engaged in the national bicycle craze. National cyclist newspapers came to cover the action. A bicycle parade began from the clubhouse and wound its way through the streets of Rockford before ending at the Nelson Hotel. The mounted bicycle police, military band and members of local and visiting bicycle clubs took part in the parade. The tournament was well attended, with no mishaps or police reports filed during the event, and the Rockford Bicycle Club secured a profit from the half-day event.

Throughout the month of July, reports about the driving park seemed dismal. Matt Maloney, who had trained a string of horses since the opening of the park, was reported to have left the driving park on July 7 to train horses in Taylor Park (located in Freeport) for the Stout Brothers' Stock Farms based in Dubuque, Iowa. In addition, D.F. Warner, an express wagon driver, decided to run his horse at the driving park to settle a five-dollar wager. After a long day of work, the horse was taken to the park to achieve a time of 3:00 or better. The *Morning Star* reported: "The steed is lame as well as overworked, and the way it was pounded and urged around the track in the hot sun of yesterday was a caution. It is certainly a case for the humane society and the unfeeling driver should be dealt with as the action deserves." It seems unlikely the horse beat the time.

On a night in late July, lightning struck a shed behind the grandstand. The fire went unnoticed until a Chicago, Milwaukee and St. Paul Railway line engineer spotted it. He pulled his whistle many times to alert people in the area. When the fire department arrived, the blaze was out of control, and not enough water was available to put it out. Hook and Ladder No. 4 responded to the scene, and in combination with heavy rain, the fire was eventually extinguished. Forty feet of sheds and meet signage were destroyed. The damage was minimal, but another fire in August resulted in a different outcome.

In mid-August, a second fire occurred. The *Rockford Daily Register Gazette* reported it was started by a careless stableman smoking a pipe. The *Rockford Daily Spectator* reported that it was started by a "tramp" who smoked around a haystack. Regardless of the actual cause, the fire destroyed a double row of 170 stalls, the blacksmith shop, barns, harnesses, sulkies, tack and a two-year-old colt worth $1,000. Unfortunately, the insurance on the driving park expired just two days before the fire. There also was no insurance on the horse, whose owner had been offered $500 for it during the previous season. George Keyt was especially upset. His prized water wagon, built to water the track when the park opened, burned in the fire. He bitterly complained in the *Rockford Morning Star* that the "worthless" oil stoves were saved from the flames, but his $300 water wagon was not. No official statement was made by the Rockford Driving Park Association as to how it would remediate losses. An autumn meet in Rockford seemed in jeopardy as other parks in Janesville, Rochelle and Washington Park (in Chicago) continued their schedules. Only shooting contests held by the Rockford Gun Club and settling bets at the Rockford Driving Park were held throughout the rest of 1893. Few horses remained stabled there for the winter months. No revenue was generated. The *Daily Register Gazette* urged the agricultural association to buy the driving park now, more than at any other time, to solve the driving park's streak of bad luck and money woes. Again, editorials suggested that the fairgrounds be converted into a public park and the driving park be reconstituted as the new fairgrounds. It was even suggested by former director Bine Sturtevant that the driving park could be cheaply bought by the city and used as a solution to the "garbage problem" that the city was currently facing. Sturtevant may not only have held frustration toward the park but also may have thought of profitable garbage collection fees. The streetcar company did not help matters, either, because on October 23, the *Daily Register Gazette* reported that the tracks that led to the park gates were removed and used elsewhere.

The lack of transportation to the park was costly, because the driving park was located outside the city limits despite housing being built nearby. To travel to the park from Rockford's downtown area, a person still could take the streetcar to the park but had to walk on Huffman Boulevard from Auburn Street all the way to Fulton and then walk another quarter-mile around the south of the track to finally arrive at the grandstand. Meanwhile, the streetcar provided riders service directly to the gate of Harlem Park—no excessive walking required.

By 1894, Rockford could boast about being home to some great horses that had been trotted across the country with very low times. Ironically, the city could not hold a race meet for them. The driving park only had one stable left that could hold twelve horses. Stockholders of the driving park became desperate. In February 1894, President L.A. Fabrick and Secretary W.H. King secured another mortgage from Andrew Gilruth for $1,900 (somehow, the first mortgage had been paid off by June 1894). That same month, the directors considered creating a village in the North End that would embrace the racetrack as its center to create its own laws. If the plan worked, the driving park could offer gambling and alcohol and avoid Rockford "blue laws" against those activities. This plan went nowhere. Others had to step in.

Ira Ginders's advertisement. *From Philippi's Rockford City Directory, A.F. Judd and Co. Book and Job Printers, 1889.*

Ira E. Ginders (who owned a livery stable and operated a hack and baggage line) and a few other horsemen put up the money and made efforts to keep training horses at the park. They first built a few new stalls in March. By April 18, a small article appeared in the *Rockford Daily Register Gazette*. Ginders and Bert Munn leased the park in order to train their horses. They sent around a subscription paper to raise funds to rebuild the stalls that had burned down the previous year. By the end of May, the stables were rebuilt, and the Rockford Driving Park Association had sold off the ten acres it owned north of Fulton Avenue for $2,500 to stay financially firm and cut its mortgage in half. In July, the driving park became the headquarters for the Rockford Bicycle Club. Members practiced on the track every evening for races held all across the Midwest. In the meantime, the owner of the streetcar railway (T.M. Ellis) decided to lease the Riverside Park baseball grounds, not far from driving park, and build a new velodrome for bicyclists there. This new track would cut the potential of any future bicycle meets being held at the driving park.

In August, editorials were written in the newspapers for and against race meets with gambling and alcohol. On September 8, Mother Nature seemed to provide her opinion on the matter when a strong gust of wind blew down the elegant front gate to the park. Rockford was not the only track to be stalled by laws against gambling and alcohol. In November, the great Rochester, New York circuit came to an end because the new state constitution prohibited pool betting at tracks. Many young and veteran trainers worked their horses at the track, but no race meets were held in 1894. Freeport's Colonel John Taylor was once again rumored to be interested in buying the track, but the *Daily Register Gazette* believed that chances were slim.

By 1895, new life was injected into the park. The High School Athletics Association decided to hold a field day, inviting all high school–aged competitors to take part in various events for no entry fee. The events must have been rained out, because they were not held until the first Saturday in May. The driving park was leased to B.C. Kimlin and C.J. Franks (a trainer who arrived at the park in January with two horses), who not only trained but also planned meets. True to their word, Kimlin and Franks held races for the first time in over a year that June.

Three races were promised on June 7 with all local horses entered. Admission was free for ladies and twenty-five cents for gentlemen. No gambling or alcohol was mentioned. There were two trotting races and one for "green" horses. The *Rockford Daily Register Gazette* reported that the event was well attended by "veteran horse watchers" and new faces alike. There were still people trying to get to the grandstand at the start of the first heat. Purses for the races were not announced. Before another race meet was held on June 20, an accident occurred. James Holmes was driving a team of horses on the track, pulling the water wagon, when they became spooked. He let go of the reins and fell off the wagon. When he fell, he bruised and tore his hip, which caused his kidney to rupture. The injury was serious, but Dr. Crawford believed that he would recover. The June 20 race meet's schedule included one trotting race, two pacing races and a "gentleman's road race" with a purse of forty dollars. Another "fair audience" attended the races, but the road race was not run due to a lack of entries.

The Fourth of July was a traditional day to hold races, because workers had the day off, yet nothing went on at the park on July 4, 1895. Rockfordians spent the holiday at Harlem Park and raced bicycles elsewhere. Meanwhile, in Freeport, the directors of their driving park arranged such a large meet in July that the *Rockford Morning Star* reported that the city made at least $200,000 in revenue. Editorials clamored for the Rockford Driving Park to do the same—and even better—since Rockford could sustain the crowds. Businessmen urged the Rockford Driving Park Association to reorganize for the good of the city, but nothing was done for the rest of the year. A spark from a passing train caused another fire that occurred along the fence line of the park, and a bet that was to be settled between men and their horses (ten dollars and the loss of the losers' horse) made the news. Lackadaisical leadership and past revenue losses were the most likely reasons for the inactivity. No one wanted to take a risk.

The 1896 Rockford Driving Park Association meeting saw the election of another new board of directors that included D.B. Redington, William Stark, J.W. Hale, B.B. Page and F.D. Root. Constant turnover in leadership seemed to be another factor in the park's downfall in addition to low attendance numbers, fires, poor weather, national economic conditions and alcohol and gambling concerns. The park had become a money pit from which recovery seemed doubtful.

In contrast, the streetcar transported passengers to the gates of Harlem Park every day during the summer months. In addition to the daily crowds, church organizations held events at Harlem Park that included picnics, speakers, baseball games, band concerts and other social activities. Some church events required special trains to transport people from surrounding areas into the park. Church groups were not the only groups to enjoy the grounds. The *Arrow* steamboat was commissioned to take forty members of the Rockford Rifles and the Mandolin Club to Harlem Park for a July 5 picnic. When a group of Illinois lawmakers came to Rockford for a visit, local officials took them to Harlem Park before dining at the Nelson Hotel. Local unions came together at Harlem Park to celebrate Labor Day.

Rockford Driving Park had limited functionality. Harlem Park was scenic, multifunctional and had a respectable reputation. The public supported Harlem Park with their patronage. Rockford Driving Park was not completely supported by the public because attendance numbers were low, and debate swirled around its reputation regarding gambling and alcohol. It was originally constructed as a park by the upper-class citizens for Rockford, and not all of the upper-class citizens would/could support the park. Since a large variety of people attended events at Harlem Park, it is remembered more widely than the driving park.

4

IS THERE A DOCTOR IN THE HOUSE?

*O*n October 1, 1896, the *Rockford Republic* reported that Frank. G. Smith, a harness-maker in the city of Rockford since 1851, had assigned his debts to George M. Blake. He was $23,000 in debt due to financial speculation and the national financial Panic of 1893. All of his stock and his business and house (assets totaling $8,000) were given to Blake. Smith also had become ill and was confined to his bed. He had been a staunch promoter of the driving park (he opened the first Rockford Driving Park Association meeting) and was a former race judge. Smith seemed to embody Rockford Driving Park. The years 1893 through 1895 were rough for the nation, which had suffered economically from the Panic of 1893, and for the park, which witnessed little in the form of horse racing. The first half of 1896 seemed no better. Again, only settling of bets on foot, a few school bicycle races and another rumor from the *Rockford Daily Register Gazette* that Fay Carney would lease the driving park if the agricultural society would buy the property and fix the grounds were reported. Just like Smith, the Rockford Driving Park was in need of care and money to support itself.

Many hoped that exciting racing on a grand scale would return to the driving park in 1897. The year's news about the park began in January with an editorial written by "Citizen" in the *Rockford Daily Register Gazette* that advised Rockford to reinvigorate the park before investing in a baseball team. There had been mention of a baseball team playing at the driving park, but the manager of the previous Rockford team lacked the funds for another team.

Rumors continued to swirl around the driving park and who would control it. The W.C. Crolius Syndicate was reportedly interested in buying or leasing the track for the right price. A representative of the syndicate was asked if the syndicate would offer "wheel" gambling at meets. The representative stated that the "wheel" had nothing to do with horse racing and deterred people from making bets on the horses. Thomas Reber, Chris Henry and Frank Wormwood were the primary men in control of the park, and they were willing to sell. Unfortunately, no deal was struck. Horses continued to train, mostly on Tuesdays and Fridays. The *Daily Register* reported that the track had escaped "ruin" and continued to be one of the best in the area. Bicycle events were held in mid-June. "A fine corn crop" and hay crop grew in the infield by August. The driving park was proving to be sporadic for events. At Harlem Park, people entered and returned again and again throughout a single season. Meanwhile, it was unique if the driving park hosted one or two events during an entire year. In February 1898, the newspapers once again ran stories about proposed race meets for the year. It seemed that the glory days of the park had come and gone, but things were about to change again.

By March 1898, Dr. H.L. McClellan had leased the driving park. He worked with Dr. Cecil in Rockford during the previous year, but no other information is known about him. The Rockford Driving Park Association seemed powerless. Another organization, the Rockford Driving Club, led by McClellan and assisted by S.C. Aagesen, had extensive plans for the park. They proposed racing meets for the summer and fall in addition to matinees, which were one-day racing events. There would not only be driving events but also a running event. Matinees of local horses were to be raced semi-monthly. Instead of offering large purses, McClellan proposed smaller ones to keep entry fees low. This would allow for more entries and local horses. Contrasted against previous leases, Dr. McClellan "retain[ed] all of the privileges connected with the driving park himself."

The newspapers commented favorably on the rebuilding of the park, which included the purchase of the old West Side Baseball Park's stands and fencing. Once the old stands were moved to the driving park, they were converted into stables to replace those that had burnt down; 150 stalls were built. A house near the park was moved inside the park grounds and converted into a clubhouse. It contained twelve rooms, and B.C. Kimlin's family (he also raced horses at the track) operated a restaurant inside. The clubhouse was chosen to take in fine views of the quarter and home stretches. Verandas were built on the ground and second floors for views toward the entire track. Newspapers conflicted about whether the clubhouse was open to the general public or only to drivers. Other park structures received new coats of paint, and other refurbishments were completed due to wear and tear that resulted from vagrants, fire and weather. The track surface had become hardened instead of springy due to its high sand content. Loam was applied to the track to remedy the problem. The Rockford Street Railway Company and the Chicago, Milwaukee and St. Paul Railway were contacted to coordinate transportation to the park.

June 2 was to be the date of the first local matinee, and July 27 was chosen as the race meets date to coincide with Elgin and Aurora's driving park schedules and for the Woodman's Picnic. Strings of horses slowly arrived in the park again. An offer of $1,800 was made for "wheel" gambling rights, but it was declined. The *Rockford Daily Register Gazette* nonchalantly commented, "In fact there will be 50 to 60 horses in training at the park in a few weeks and it will look like old times."

In May and June 1898, the newspapers were abuzz about the driving park. McClellan had brought the park to life at a considerable monetary cost but also a personal one. On May 7, the *Rockford Republic* reported that McClellan was working on a rafter of a building in the park when the wood gave way. He could still walk, but with difficulty. Despite the accident, his injury did not prevent him from personally advertising the driving park in Oregon, Illinois, in mid-May. The clubhouse and grounds were nearing completion, and twenty-five stalls were completed.

Gimmicks were not new for meets, and McClellan arranged one for his opening day. John Lawson, known as the "Terrible Swede," was to race his bicycle against horses in a five-mile race. He had successfully performed this style of race before in the employ of Buffalo Bill. As a promotional stunt, Lawson raced against horses at the park on May 13, just weeks before the big day of races on June 2. Lawson must have easily won again, because the *Daily Register Gazette* reported that the jockeys could not induce the horses to run. The race must have been an utter disappointment, since McClellan stated in the paper that the June 2 races would prove far more exciting than this warm-up gimmick race.

On June 2, the weather was clear and fair. The driving park had competition for spectators from a variety of other events. There was a "Ladies' Ball Game" at Riverside Park. The Woodman's Picnic was being held on the fairgrounds. Harlem Park was open. The crowds (several thousand at twenty-five cents admission per person) gathered at the driving park to see good racing, and they were not disappointed. There were no

John Lawson, the "Terrible Swede." *Courtesy of Richard Arthur Norton.*

disputes, false starts or accidents. The entries came from around the area, including Rochelle, Durand and Paw Paw. The future for a larger meet was looking bright. A four-day race meet was planned for July, with a total purse of $10,000, and three races were scheduled for each day. New "strings" of horses were shipped to the park each week and trained leading up to the event. However, the specter of alcohol-related accusations came to the fore again.

Off the track, drama once again unfolded. The North End Rockford WCTU (Woman's Christian Temperance Union) had concerns about the park. McClellan was invited to speak about the park's operations at the group's monthly meeting, and he reassured the women that operations were acceptable. However, according to the *Rockford Daily Register Gazette*, warrants were filed against B.C. Kimlin, McClellan and two others for alcohol sales in the clubhouse during the races on June 2. A journalist from the *Rockford Morning Star* wrote that a private detective named Hearst was employed by the Civic Federation to go undercover to the driving park to observe their operations. According to Hearst, he witnessed the sale of liquor to minors at the clubhouse. Kimlin stated that no liquor was sold at the clubhouse, and the only minor in the clubhouse was brought in by Hearst. Kimlin and the others were released after questioning. McClellan was out of town watching racing in Woodstock and did not have a statement. Throughout newspaper articles, there was a prevailing feeling that the North End Rockford WCTU had organized this "bust" through the Civic Federation. Liquor-law violators would face harsh punishment.

State's attorney Arthur H. Frost sent word to Judge L.L. Morrison that he could not find enough evidence to bring a case against McClellan and the others. R.K. Welsh was hired for the defense. Kimlin and others were held for $100 bond by the grand jury. On July 11, ninety-two people signed a petition to ban liquor sales at driving park. The petition was placed in front of the Winnebago County Board of Supervisors, which tabled it because the driving park had not taken out a liquor license. The irony was that the board adjourned early to see the matinee races being held at the park on that very day.

Other legal troubles developed for McClellan. The Home Building and Loan Association brought a suit against him to replevin the home that was moved into the park to become the clubhouse. The Rockford Lumber and Fuel Company added to the suit charges of $372.50 for unpaid building materials delivered to the park from May 6 through May 20. The Rockford Driving Club, Emily Graham and Clara Hill were also defendants in the suit. The driving club stated that they simply allowed McClellan to make improvements, and the ladies were included as mortgagees of the property. Due to the pressure of these legal troubles and various monetary concerns, McClellan cancelled the upcoming race meet that was scheduled; however, training continued through the month of July. There were 248 horses entered for the events, but McClellan was unsure that the meet would be profitable because, once again, he could not provide the "privileges" that normally accompanied racing at other tracks. The journalist who covered the story painted doom and gloom over the park by stating, "It is understood that the clubhouse will be vacated and driving park closed up. Dr. McClellan has gone to considerable expense in improvements about the park, which he will lose." Kimlin left for Ohio to race his horses there. By the end of the month, talk of the agricultural society holding its annual fair at the driving park again swirled. It was believed that people associated with the driving park agitated this old debate. After 1898, Dr. H.L. McClellan disappeared from the newspapers and was never again listed in the Rockford City Directories. He left town and never appeared in court.

On August 11, the Home Building and Loan Association's contractor, Mr. Wayland, and police officers entered the park to forcefully remove the clubhouse. Kimlin was in Ohio at the time and was unaware of the move. Friends tried to secure his personal property from the clubhouse in his absence. Dr. B.B. Page, the secretary of the Rockford Driving Park Association, was urged to stop the process, but the clubhouse was removed on rollers anyway. Meanwhile, horse racing was held at the fairgrounds that month with many horses that had either trained or raced at driving park. In September, the Freeport Taylor Driving Park heavily advertised its race meet in the Rockford newspapers.

Bicyclists returned to the park in the absence of horses. Harry Needham decided to attempt to break the city mile record at driving park instead of the fairgrounds (where his attempt was originally announced) because the driving park's track was banked better. On September 11, Needham rode his bicycle around the mile-long track in one minute and fifty-nine seconds, setting a new record. T.J. Malana was a unique cyclist with another plan. His business was full of rats. He usually drowned them or set his terrier on them. Malana was also a marksman and decided to dispose of the rats in a more unique and entertaining way. While at driving park, he released rats he had trapped at his business and shot them while riding on the back of a tandem bicycle pedaled by an assistant. Apparently, the bicycle was rigged with "training wheels" so it would not fall over during the heat of the hunt.

By February 1899, the lawsuit between McClellan and the Rockford Lumber and Fuel Company was settled. As one court case closed, another opened. Emily Graham and Clara Hill sued the Rockford Driving Club for their court fees and for the amount that was left on their original 1892 mortgage. A total of $2,101.33 in damages against the Rockford Driving Club was sought solely by Graham. The Rockford Driving Club still owed Hill $3,077, too.

Another "savior" was approached by the Rockford Driving Club to get them out of a financial disaster and to lead them toward a brighter future. Charles Hancock, who operated the Nutwood Driving Park in Dubuque, Iowa, was the chairman of the Republican State Committee and a leading businessman. He was interested in leasing the Rockford Driving Park if the conditions were right (meaning that they involved gambling and alcohol). He stated that he would invest $3,000 in improvements and bring $50,000 to Rockford merchants during race meets. He was scheduled to visit Rockford in late February in order to investigate the conditions of the track after attending a horse auction in Chicago. The newspapers were filled with reasons why Rockford should encourage Hancock's lease. Even former mayor Amasa Hutchins believed that Hancock's lease, with protections against "blue laws," would be good for the city. Nonetheless, no reports were made of Hancock coming to Rockford.

The Rockford Driving Club was officially in default. There was no light, no hope, no way of getting out of the jam as it had somehow previously managed to do. On November 1, 1900, a public sale was held for the driving park. Emily Graham and Clara Hill were the highest bidders, and at the end of the sale, Graham held the title completely. The sound of hoofbeats against the sandy-loam track seemed like a fading memory. Even Dr. McClellan could not save his dying driving park "patient" due to his lack of funding and community support.

5.

"SPEEDY EVENTS FOR THE PUFF WAGONS AT DRIVING PARK"

*T*he year was 1904. No events had been held at the park for six years. The Rockford Driving Park Association and the Rockford Driving Club were practically defunct. Chicago showman H.M. Shoub stirred the first glimmer of hope for activity in the park when he wanted to run temporary railroad tracks from the west end ballpark to the driving park to have a spectacular engine collision. The spectacle had drawn huge crowds in Chicago before, and he thought that he could draw huge crowds to Rockford by repeating the stunt with fireworks on July 4. To pay for all of this entertainment, Shoub solicited local manufacturers, who undoubtedly turned him away because his plans did not come to fruition. Meanwhile, in Beloit, the driving park there announced that it would offer $500 in trotting and pacing purses during their July 4 celebrations. However, the Rockford Driving Park would soon be witness to a new version of horsepower on its track.

Automobiles developed in the 1890s and were owned by the upper classes because they were constructed by hand. Most automobile producers were former carriagemakers, and very few, like White and Buick, made other things. Henry Ford did not develop his famous assembly line manufacturing until 1913. However, the automobile became more affordable for the masses as years passed and gave the driving park new life.

Mentions of automobiles in Rockford first began to appear in Rockford newspapers in 1903. The newspapers randomly called automobiles "horseless carriages" or "puff wagons," but not cars. Drivers were sometimes called "chauffeurs." Rockford industrialists, just as they had owned/trained horses to race in the previous decade, had the means of owning these cutting-edge machines. Subsequently, so many of them owned early automobiles that a club was formed, just as the Rockford Driving Park Association had formed in the 1800s.

On August 25, the Rockford Automobile Club (RAC) leased the driving park from Julius Graham (Emily Graham's husband and himself a member of the RAC) until December 1 with the extended option of leasing it further for three to five years. The club was interested in hosting auto races on the grounds for two days in September or October. Local and non-local drivers were invited, and all race finish times were made official by the American Automobile Association (AAA). In preparation, a city grader leveled the track, and a crew of workers removed weeds. Every Saturday afternoon, the club opened the park for an open basket picnic for members and nonmembers alike in order to generate interest in the meet.

On September 8, after the RAC met at the Everett Barnes Auto Agency (an automobile dealership), the club published a schedule of events in the newspapers. These races were the first of their kind in Rockford. A fifty-mile nonstop race was to be the main attraction, with a three-mile race for women drivers and the first motorcycle race scheduled on the second day. Winners of the events received various automobile-related prizes or medals. Gimmicks were once again considered to draw crowds, because the club was interested in bringing the "Bullet" and "999" (which broke the half-mile track record in Aurora) cars to their meet, but there was concern that the owners' schedules would not work. A set of "stairs" was built for cars to attempt to "climb" in case the other gimmicks did not work.

Excitement grew. Newspapers outside of Rockford promoted the races. Buttons were proudly worn by the forty-five club members. Posters were pasted on fences. Dwight P. Cutler issued a challenge that his air-cooled Knox Car would beat Elmer Ward's Winton in the fifty-mile race. The loser would pay a dollar for every minute it lagged behind. Dwight Cutler's father, Asa E. Cutler, was no stranger to the park. In 1891, he instigated the end to gambling and drinking at the park, so it was ironic that his son proposed this wager thirteen years later. The *Rockford Republic* generated excitement not only from a racing standpoint, but also from a feminine perspective. A journalist in the September 12 issue of the paper claimed that the race meet would be great for women to attend so they could show off their new gowns. Milady designed new gowns, and Ashton's windows filled with auto apparel. The bicycle craze of the 1890s had changed women's fashion, and the automobile craze changed women's fashion again. Meanwhile, in the days leading up to the meet, local drivers practiced on the track to see how their machines handled the course.

Everything was positive until the night of September 25. At seven o'clock that evening, a damaging storm hit Rockford and caused widespread destruction. The streetcar company suffered $2,000 in damages to its equipment. Telephone wires burnt out or became disconnected. Barns and chimneys were blown over. Entire roofs were blown off, windows were broken and fallen trees made some streets impassable. The grandstand at Riverside Baseball Park completely lifted off the ground and overturned on the other side of the park fence. At the Westside Cemetery (Greenwood), there were many trees blown over on top of grave markers. The driving park did not escape damage, either. Strong winds destroyed portions of the fence and many of the outbuildings. The *Daily Register Gazette* could not confirm it was a tornado, but many believed it was possible. The east side of Rockford had not been affected by the storm. The west side of the city was "crippled," and the cleanup process had to begin.

On the morning of the first day of races, October 7, a parade of thirty automobiles, led by E.C. Dunn and his dog, slowly wound its way through the streets of Rockford beginning at Cole's garage. Each car was decorated or hung local merchant advertisements. Since the streetcar track had been removed from Huffman Boulevard leading to the park, buses met streetcars on Main Street to transport people to the park gates. The military band agreed to play between races. Admission to the park was twenty-five cents, and advanced tickets could be bought at Porter's or at Worthington and Slade's on the east side. Spectators could buy a hot sandwich and a cigar from Lloyd Osmus. No alcohol sales or gambling wheels were mentioned.

A week before the races, the club members had attended the Chicago race meet. They hoped that they could draw a "record-breaker" to attend the Rockford races. They were successful in recruiting W.T. Muir. He drove a twenty-four-horsepower machine and was considered a "professional race driver." The famous "999" car was to appear in Rockford, but its owner, Jed Newkirk, cancelled the night before the Rockford races. He had entered his car elsewhere. No matter, as attendance for the first day of racing reached around six hundred spectators.

The first race was a five-mile race for gas-powered automobiles. It was to start at 1:30 p.m. but was delayed for thirty minutes because some of the contestants had not shown up on time. This was possibly due to mechanical issues, because during the race, two (Dr. Dunn and Ad Burr) out of the five cars had mechanical issues and did not finish. Yet, races were won and lost. Afterward, drivers boasted and challenged each other. Elmer Ward, for example, challenged Dwight Cutler by stating, "I will race Cutler again for 50, 100 or 300 miles, or any other distance under the same conditions." Cutler replied, "This car was never run an inch before six o'clock this morning and isn't worked out yet. I would like to meet Ward a week or two later, after I have a chance to work my machine out a little."

The *Morning Star* concluded that if people were skeptical of the power and capabilities of automobiles before the races, they were believers afterward. The times were faster than expected, but they possibly could have been faster had it not been for the high winds. The spectators were not pleased with the winds, either, because dust coated their faces as the automobiles blazed past the grandstand.

Ten races were run on the second day. The main event was the fifty-mile race between Ward's and Cutler's machines. Ward beat Cutler by almost six minutes (76:20 to 82:12). At the beginning, Cutler's lightweight automobile was faster than Ward's, and for twenty miles, it was debatable who would be victorious. Subsequently, Ward began to lap Cutler's machine. The spectators in the grandstand gave Ward a standing ovation. Cutler began to make excuses about how he had just installed his automobile's water-cooled engine that morning and that Ward had a mechanic (Mr. Schenck) onboard who tended to every part of the vehicle. A rumor started that Ward did not drive his own automobile and that he drove a Winton direct from the Chicago plant. There was no mention of money exchanged between the two as they were pressed by the crowd after the race, but it was expected that Cutler advanced Ward five dollars and some odd change.

Automobiles were nicknamed "devil wagons," but this did not stop two fearless female drivers from racing at driving park. After the fifty-mile road race was finished, two women entered the race for women drivers: Laverne Cole and Lorena Day. The women practiced driving their Ramblers in the park for weeks before the race. Each time they practiced racing against each other, they had crossed the finish line almost side-by-side. Day beat Cole's Rambler by what seemed to be inches, as shown in the staged picture. The *Morning Star* believed that Day won because, in the last ten feet before the finish line, Day stood up and "lurched forward with all of her might" just enough to push her automobile to victory. It was noted by the *Rockford Republic* that the Rockford women's times were faster than the women's times posted in Chicago a week before.

Laverne Cole and Lorena Day crossed the finish line in almost a dead heat. *From the Rockford Chamber of Commerce, 1912.*

A motorcycle race was run after the ladies had their exciting race. At the time, motorcycles did not have kick-starters and basically were bicycles with engines. Riders were pushed into a rolling start and then followed a pace motorcycle for a lap. Once the warm-up lap was completed and the riders were mostly lined up at the starting line, the race began. Fred J. Jastrom, on his Mitchell motorcycle, finished the race in first place.

The meet netted a profit of $300, which was divided amongst the club members. The *Rockford Republic* beamed: "That such an amount should be profited by the first meet goes to show that auto racing is successful in this city in a financial way. It will doubtless lead to larger machines and regular race meets." It was the first time that the driving park had seen a profit in thirteen years—since its opening glory days in 1891.

On October 10, the *Rockford Republic* announced that several of the local drivers decided to race each other again. Notable winners were challenged by close losers who wanted to prove themselves. Frank Ulrici was challenged by Everett Barnes. A.W. Church, Dr. E.C. Dunn, Dwight Cutler and Fred Cutler all could not seem to get enough racing. Laverne Cole even challenged Elmer Ward to a fifty-mile race. However, none of the races was recorded in the newspapers, because all of them were unofficial. A.E. Henry, a local jeweler, could not get enough racing, either. On October 18, the *Rockford Republic* announced that a ten-mile handicap would be sponsored by the RAC for cars that were driven on the streets of Rockford. He wanted to compare and contrast the durability/sustainability of each of the automobiles (possibly to see what kind of automobile he would eventually buy for himself). Henry agreed to offer a "golden loving cup" to the winner.

Despite the success of the two-day meet, negativity filled the newspapers following it. On October 9, a *Morning Star* writer wrote that he had attended the driving park's opening days and was startled to see that people bet on the auto races just like they had on the horses. He also found it interesting that the people who went to court "to put an end to racing in Rockford" were doing the same kind of activities that were thought to be "bad" for Rockford at the auto races. On October 10, the *Rockford Republic* included an article entitled, "The Old Driving Park War." The writer claimed that there were no people involved with ending the gambling and liquor selling enterprises at the auto races during the previous days. The writer literally called out the *Morning Star* and fellow *Republic* journalists by calling their pieces "fables." The article stated that "if" people who had a hand in stopping the "openly illegalities" were at the park for the auto races, they should be praised instead of denounced, because they had the courage to stop them. In addition, the horse races had legal betting pools; it was the "wheel" and the shell games that were illegal—and neither was played at the auto races.

Automobile fever gripped Rockford. On October 13, the *Rockford Daily Register Gazette* reported on a new proposed automobile racetrack to be built along the streetcar rail lines and Harlem Park. The new track would be built on donated land if the RAC promised to maintain the use of the land. The reasons behind the new park were many and historical. The streetcar tracks no longer reached the driving park gates. The grandstand was on the other side of the park from the gates, which made for a long walk to the grandstand. Some club members did not want to refurbish the "old" driving park. The new site had a slight incline, but supporters believed that the ground would eventually be leveled. The plan was never carried out.

By February 1905, the RAC had announced it would host another racing meet on July 4. The RAC believed it had enough time to improve the track's condition to better than it had been for the October 1904 meet, and the club could encourage more professional drivers to attend. Either Julius Graham, owner of the park grounds, was not made aware of these plans, or he simply could not negotiate enough money. Graham leased the entire park for farming purposes, which he could legally do, since the RAC's lease expired at the end of 1904. The Beloit Driving Park noticed the RAC's predicament and began negotiations with the club. Graham was given many offers by the RAC, but he refused them all. To add to the RAC's misery, the Rockford

Streetcar Company stated that it would not consider rebuilding a line to the driving park gates.

The decision to lease the driving park out to farmers also affected local high school sports. The Rockford High School track team could not practice at the fairgrounds because they were all plowed up. The driving park was too far away from the school. As a result, no athletes were sent to Springfield to participate in the state meet because they lacked a training area.

The *Rockford Republic* announced that a group of horsemen called the Matinee Association was to hold "ice races" on the frozen Rock River. They equipped their horses with sleds, and local businessmen offered mostly horse blankets, whips and cigars to the winners. The "ice speedway" horse races must have been a success, because the group of horsemen offered to help the RAC in negotiations with Graham. However, this was to no avail. Graham's fee was still $150 too high. The 1905 racing season was slipping away. Crops grew in the driving park's infield. The RAC had no other option but to hold its races in Beloit. The owners of the Interurban Line were pleased, and fifteen thousand spectators were expected to witness the events on July 4. Instead of the economic impact being felt in Rockford, Beloit businesses would reap the gains, because Graham would not budge. Another race season at driving park wasted away.

6.

HORSE RACING RETURNS

*O*n August 5, 1905, the *Rockford Morning Star* reported that the Rockford Driving Park Association was going to be "born again." Area horsemen, led by William W. Bennett, were tired of the inertia and formed a new driving club. Membership climbed to sixty-five, then ninety dues-paying members (annual dues were ten dollars) and could peak at one hundred. The club proposed negotiations with Julius Graham, and if they failed, the members considered buying land to build another driving park. The park's track was still in good condition, and the grandstand still stood, but the barns had all burned down.

In the remaining weeks of August, a deal was struck with the farmer who leased the land from Graham. Work was furiously carried out. The first official morning exercises were held on August 29, but Fay Carney could not wait and trotted his horses around the graders as they worked. The stables were quickly rebuilt, because there were suddenly fourteen trainers from around the Midwest who wanted to train at the park. Enthusiasm for reopening the park for horse racing even made *Horse World*, a national magazine, take notice.

The *Rockford Republic* claimed that there were at least ten horsemen willing to invest between $500 and $1,000 into a "Fair Driving Club," bringing the starting capital up to $10,000. Despite the "easy money" collected, there were issues. For one, the new members of the association had to determine whether or not they were to have simply horse racing or include exhibits, sideshows or carnivals to make their events more family-friendly. The new association also continued to bargain with Graham and the streetcar company for better terms and conditions. In the meantime, the new Rockford Driving Park Association announced that a matinee race was to be held on September 26. The details would eventually work themselves out.

The first detail was the date itself, which was moved from September 26 to September 29 due to the need for more time to advertise and promote the races. The second was: What to do? The association settled on having three harness races and an oddball mule race that would feature local celebrities driving the mules. There were also pony and saddle show events for children. The prizes were all donated from local businesses and varied from five dollars in gold from the association to boxes of candy for the children's classes. Many of the prizes were put on display in the Keeling Drug Store windows to generate advertising for local businesses and for attending the benefit races. The gate entry for spectators was free, but donations to St. Anthony Hospital were encouraged. In the days leading up to the matinee races, the newspapers speculated on the winners, and the mule contestants "trash-talked" about their animals—but nature had other ideas.

On September 28, it had rained heavily. The journalists shrugged it off and thought that the track would be perfect for racing the next day. The clouds refused to part. The matinee races were called off and rescheduled for the following Wednesday. Paul Schuster, one of the two mule-racers, made light of the situation. He was quoted in the *Republic* as being sorry that they were cancelled because he knew that a large group of people was going to see the mule race and that he was afraid of Tom Reber's (his competitor) mule dying of old age before the race could be run.

Finally, race day came. The infield was filled with carriages and a few automobiles. The grandstand slowly filled with people proudly wearing their ribbons as they waited in anticipation. The first events were show driving events for both men and women drivers. All three of the driving races were run cleanly. The only injury of the day was to Katherine Watkins, who fell from her pony after her saddle's girth broke. She was treated at St. Anthony Hospital (which made sense) and was released with minor bruises.

Tom Reber drove his faithful mule S.S. ("Stinking Springs") to the line with a flake of hay dangled from a pole just out of the reach of S.S.'s mouth. Schuster dressed as an auto racer. Three heats were raced; Reber and Schuster each won one, and the first heat was a draw—so the race winner was a draw. Schuster accused a villain of chloroforming his mule and replacing it with a decrepit imposter. He did not accuse Reber of doing such things because he believed that Reber was an honest man.

St. Anthony Hospital received $800 during the event, and a good time was had by all. Everything was roses again…but vandals had other plans for the park. Only two weeks after the matinee event, vandals began to attack the park's buildings and vehicles. Charles Wilson's speed cart was destroyed. The wheels, thrills and seat were broken, and parts of the cart were thrown on a shed's roof. A copper boiler used to heat horse water tanks was riddled with bullet holes. The vandals attempted to gain access to the stables by ripping a door off its hinges. Charles Atwood's stable windows were all shattered (which was not the first time this had been done). The costs of the damages were not exactly reported, but they were considerable.

The roller coaster continued. On November 1, the press reported that a new Winnebago County Fair Association was to be funded, and the annual fairs were to be held at the driving park. This had been a longstanding vision, and at the end of 1906, it became a strong possibility. The *Rockford Morning Star* claimed $10,000 were easily being raised, a ten-year lease was negotiated for the driving park, new improvements were to be made and the fair would be better than the Oregon, Belvidere or Beloit fairs. By the end of the month, the Winnebago County Fair Association had raised $12,000 and held a meeting with the Rockford Driving Park Association. The Rockford Street and Interurban Railway Company also took notice of the new vitality and began to consider replacing the loop track that led to the park gates. Snow began to fall. The time to plan was now, before it was too late.

In March 1907, Julius Graham once again ended the momentum as he denied access to the park. Graham placed "too many barriers," such as property taxes, in front of the fair association, and a deal was never made. Originally, Graham verbally agreed that he would pay the first five years of property taxes for the park, then the fair association would pay the last five years of a ten-year lease. Later, Graham changed his mind and informed the fair association that it should pay for all ten years of property taxes, all of the legal fees to secure the lease and for any other legal matters that could arise from activities held at the park. These conditions proved to be too much for the fair association. To accentuate the deal's demise, in late March, a section of stalls burned to the ground, supposedly due to a careless hobo. If a deal could have been struck between the Winnebago County Agricultural Fair Association and Graham, the driving park area may have looked very different today.

The fair association was unable to hold the fair at the park, but the Rockford Amateur Driving Club maintained its lease with Graham and kept it busy. In April, the driving club announced that it would hold a two-

This possible Charles Atwood–owned stable was located on Latham Street east of Rockford Driving Park. *Photograph by the author.*

The building that was possibly a stable was torn down in 2017 and became a parking lot. *Photograph by the author.*

day benefit meet for the Rockford Elks Club on June 6. Admission to the races would be charged, but no prize money was guaranteed. The National Trotting Association would record the race times, and W.W. Bennett, C.H. Wilson and Harry Richardson were slated as being the starters. Richardson was in charge of making the track ready for the upcoming race season, and Charles Atwood was quick to have seven to eight horses stabled at the park only five days after the June meet announcement. Ed O'Connor actively trained his horses as well, but weather yet again prevented progress. The daily temperatures were too low and foiled Richardson's attempts to bank the track, and Atwood kept his horses inside their stable and out of the snow.

The weather caused the club to postpone the June 6 meet for the Elks to June 19. The cold temperatures prevented the horses from being trained in time for it. According to the *Rockford Daily Register*, there were at least a dozen horses trained, but only half of them were fast. On June 19, the club again postponed the meet, because the horses lacked enough training time due to the cold weather. The *Rockford Republic* joked that "the weatherman ought to be horsewhipped." The club rescheduled the meet again for the July 4 holiday weekend.

A *Republic* headline on June 22 questioned: "Will the Races for July Fourth Be Called Off?" The newspaper was concerned because no entries had been filed for the meet just days before the deadline. The journalist believed that the horses were evenly matched, and the owners wanted to avoid loses. The *Republic* later assured its readers that the meet would be held, because trainers finally entered their horses. D. Fay Carney supposedly trained "Spot Cash" so hard that he nearly killed the horse. Charles Atwood's horse apparently ate his entry fee. He reportedly shouted to call the veterinarian. A stable boy shouted back, "Send for the YMCA campaigners. They can get money out of anything." Atwood entered with other cash on hand.

On July 4, the track was in good condition, and the horses pulled along their drivers in morning workouts. Around 1,400 people spent their holiday at the races. Admission was twenty-five cents. The Forest City band entertained the crowd between race heats. There were two pace races and one trotting. Each race had at least five horses (the minimum to run a race). The program was printed in the *Morning Star* on June 30, so race favorites had been debated. No alcohol or gambling was reported. The races were all won in straight heats.

The year 1907 was a presidential election year. Theodore Roosevelt's central domestic policy was termed the "Square Deal." The secretary of the

Amateur Driving Club, W.W. Bennett, advertised the July 4 meet with the slogan, "Every heat a horse race and a square deal to all." The driver Harry Cassidy noticed that one of the horses entered in the 2:20 pace race was not exactly what it seemed. Cassidy drove Billy Sunday and noticed that one of the horses he competed against paced under a different name (Seedless was actually a horse named Onward Star) to win by outranking his competition. Cassidy's inquiry swayed the judges, and the horse was removed from the race card. Onward Star's driver, despite his deception, was allowed to pace solo for a matinee track record and succeeded by two seconds at 2:18.

The success of the July 4 matinee prompted the club to hold another matinee on July 24. They decided to host four races—one hobbled pacing, one nonhobbled pacing, one "green" pacing and one free-for-all trot—and changed the format. Instead of winning two out of three heats to win a race, they decided races were to be won best three out of five heats. Admission doubled to fifty cents, but the horses were in the best shape they had ever been in, because they were about to leave Rockford for circuit racing in August. George Keyt, in his red necktie and horseshow stick pin, was interviewed by the *Republic* about the upcoming July 24 races. He stated that the races were very evenly matched and reminisced about Bine Sturtevant's Wisconsin King, Frank Smith's Chief and Dan Carney's string of horses. In addition, he gave D. Fay Carney some advice about driving his horse Spot Cash to the front sometime.

On the morning of July 24, it rained but soon cleared. Spectators and drivers were pleased, because the races would commence, and flying dust was kept low. The rye in the infield had been cut, so everybody could see the horses. The *Republic* reported that the military band played "hoarse [*sic*] music" downtown and then boarded streetcars to the driving park to entice attendance. At two o'clock, five hundred spectators anxiously anticipated the start of the first race. They were not disappointed. In last heat of the first race, "D. Fay Carney and Harry Cassidy drove their horses so hard" that only a piece of tissue paper could separate the noses of their horses Spot Cash and Hazel M., respectively. The heat was declared a draw. Hazel M. was declared the race winner due to her previous heat placings. Cassidy won the second race as well, against two different horses owned by Charles Atwood. Colleta O. had a difficult time because one of the wheels on Cassidy's sulky broke, but he maintained control of the horse and was still able to prevail.

As the days were growing shorter and the excitement of the July 24 races lingered, the drivers of the previous month's races wanted to race one more time before temperatures changed. The driving club agreed that another day of races would be held on August 7. The rains had again proved to be useful, and more horses had been entered, which meant that they could hold more races. While horsemen trained their steeds and paid entry fees, Everett K. Barnes finished building his "horseless carriage" and set out to break the mile track record. Arthur Gardiner had set the track record of 1:17 during the 1904 automobile race meet. Roy Harrington drove Barnes's automobile around the track in 1:14. Harrington believed that he could have gone faster if the northwest corner of the track was not so tight and in better condition. A few days later, Louis Gorham Harrison challenged this record and claimed that he had driven around the track in 1:12 during the race meet in 1904. Once records were checked, Harrison's objection was confirmed. The title was to be shared.

The August 7 matinee races were filled with excitement, but all of the races were won in straight heats. The *Daily Register Gazette* complained that despite another good show of horseflesh, Rockford citizens failed to attend in great numbers. The journalist explained that the original Rockford Driving Park Association disbanded due to the lack of attendance, and that it would be shameful if history repeated itself.

The track became silent. There was talk of one last race meet for 1907 if the weather held, but nothing was done. In December, a new form of "racing" was discussed. It appeared that some Rockfordians began to bet each other on how far and how fast they could walk. M.A. Benson, who worked at the E&W Store, proclaimed that he could walk seven miles in an hour and could walk from Rockford to Byron in three hours. Frank J. O'Brien bet Ed O'Connor ten dollars that he could walk from Rockford to Byron in three and a half hours. O'Connor believed that he could not achieve that distance and time in four and a half hours. Stanton Hyer also believed that he could walk seven miles in an hour but did not want to prove it by walking the driving park track. He thought it would be too monotonous. The post office became involved, too. Albert Smith or F.H. Cronk were alleged to be the fastest walkers, but Louis Linberg wanted to represent the postmen. The other postmen discounted Linberg because he claimed to have knocked a wild goose from the sky by throwing a rock at it. W.W. Bennett chimed in and suggested that a walking contest be held at the driving park to validate all of the boasts. A small admission fee would be charged, and a charity could benefit.

The walking "fad" took root. Throughout the month of December, many Rockford citizens could be seen speedily walking the track at the driving park or the old fairgrounds. Friends of O'Connor and O'Brien pressured them to walk from Rockford to Winnebago and back for a cash prize. They even suggested that an automobile drive slowly alongside in case one became tired and could no longer walk. The men declined. Arthur Crumb and Bennett actually started training against each other. Crumb roused Bennett out of bed at six in the morning. They then walked from Bennett's house to the driving park to determine each other's abilities as Bennett kept time on his stopwatch. He was amazed at how fast he and Crumb had walked until he noticed that his stopwatch's second hand had become entangled with the minute hand and stopped working. Not discouraged, the two walked to the starting line of the track and began to walk. Crumb took the lead. They continued on through the gates of the park and walked all the way back to Bennett's house. That's when Crumb noticed that his pedometer was not working, either. They agreed to have Elisha Thayer repair their broken equipment and again attempt to settle their bets.

In January 1908, the Rockford Amateur Driving Club met to discuss the upcoming year. The driving park track was the center of attention. Some members proposed changing the dynamic from a mile-long track into a half-mile track. Most of the circuit tracks were half-mile tracks, and racing on a half-mile track was more exciting than on a mile track. There were also members who demanded that an entirely new track and park should be built instead; a proposed site was located just south of Harlem Park. The Auburn Street Bridge and streetcars were nearby, the soil was good enough, the hillside could be used for seating and the crowds from Harlem Park could easily see the races. A smaller contingent raised the notion of returning racing to the fairgrounds, but the city would probably not allow it and Kent Creek would have to be bridged in at least two places. The Rockford Amateur Driving Club was not the only "family" looking for a new home in the winter.

The Earlywine family comprised two adult males, one adult female and several children. They owned four wagons and eleven horses. They had traveled north and planned to stay in Dixon. Due to the favorable weather, the Earlywines decided to continue northward. They reached Rockford and stopped at the driving park in February because of extreme cold weather. The Earlywines rented one of the remaining barns because it was big enough to shelter all of their horses and their large family. A *Morning Star* journalist visited the park to get the "scoop." He immediately saw the children playing outside the barn on an ice pond while wearing hardly enough clothing to keep warm. Once the journalist entered the barn, he noticed that the living area was very small and unkempt. The family spoke English and informed the journalist that they were not gypsies but of German descent and were traveling to Northern Wisconsin to stay with relatives. The journalist must not have believed their story, because he believed that they were nomadic and lived by selling and trading horses. They intended to stay in the barn until March or whenever the weather allowed them to continue traveling.

Another group of people who made the driving park their home was the Rockford High School track and field team. The team had left their equipment in a shed, and on April 19, 1908, the thief or thieves broke into it and stole thirty-five dollars of equipment. The track team had been plagued by past thefts, but some members believed they knew who did it and worked with school officials and the police. The timing of the theft was unfortunate, because a track meet between the juniors and seniors was to be held later that week. The winners of the twelve events advanced to compete in the Beloit track meet later in May.

In April, the association met at Ed O'Connor's offices in the Ashton Block. W.W. Bennett's business required him to be absent from club activities for extended time, so he declined reinstatement. A half-mile track conversion was again a topic of discussion. More local horses were to be stabled and trained at the park. Many stockholders attended the meeting and were satisfied that another successful season would come to fruition despite the track's length, the need for buses to transport people from the streetcar to the gate and the grandstand's distance from the gate.

The Rockford Amateur Driving Club took no chances with the weather (like it did in 1907). The first matinee racing day was set for July 4. Familiar characters reappeared for another racing season despite continuous rains. On June 30, horses were stabled at the park. "Pray for good weather," was the sentiment of a *Morning Star* journalist. As with many previous articles, the *Morning Star* claimed that the July 4 matinee races promised new records and fast horses. Rains made the track "heavy." A double-header baseball game was to be played at Riverside Park between Rockford and Oshkosh. Many churches and other social groups celebrated the holiday with picnics. Harlem Park owners promised special programs in the auditorium in the afternoon and the evening, culminating with fireworks. However, admission to the horse races was only twenty-five cents, and the grandstand and transportation to it was free.

Men furiously worked with dredges the previous day and all throughout the morning of July 4. The race start was delayed due to the wet track, but hundreds patiently waited and discussed the new, fashionable dresses in the crowd. In the first pacing event, Miss Rex won the race by winning all three

RACING, POLITICS & CIRCUSES

RACES TO ATTRACT BIG CROWD TODAY

PREPARATIONS FOR FINE MATI-NEE AT DRIVING PARK.

HORSES IN FINE FORM

Will Be Sent at Their Best and No Races Will Be Hippodromes—First Test of the Steppers Since Spring Training.

Among the places of especial interest for today, and which is likely to attract a large number of persons is the driving park, where the initial matinee under the auspices of the Amateur Driving club will be given. Some of the horsemen have been awaiting this event for weeks as it will be the real test of the horses which have been given tryouts at the park for the past few weeks.

The rivalry which has sprung up is intense, and the events to be decided this afternoon will be real horse races

IS ONE OF THE BEST

H. W. BUCKBEE'S RED KING,
Who Will Fight Spot Cash for Honors Today.

H.W. Buckbee's horse Red King. *From "Is One of the Best,"* Morning Star, *July 4, 1908.*

heats (although the mare had bulked and thrown her driver into the track the previous week during training). In the second race, Cerilla won the race in three straight heats (though the last heat could have been considered a dead heat between Cerilla and Black Bird). The third free-for-all race was by far the most exciting. Red King and Spot Cash were tightly one-and-two for all three heats. Red King's driver probably felt Spot Cash's hot breath down the back of his collar. The attendance reached into the hundreds, and automobiles and carriages alike had been parked in the infield near the homestretch for the entire afternoon. All of the horses' owners and drivers split the winnings and seemed pleased.

In September, the park again hosted racing. This time, it hosted another variety of "steed." Motorcycles originally raced in 1904 were to be raced again on the morning of September 13, 1908. Local riders could lap the mile track in a minute or a second or two below. Motorcycle races were held on September 27. Horsemen could care less and demanded that the Rockford Amateur Driving Club host one more horse-racing matinee before it was too late. Horses were returning from out-of-state circuits, so the time was right. Days passed. Nothing was done. The year ended quietly with news of R.T. Pierce's lease of the land in December 1909 for farming purposes. Pierce must have farmed the infield but left the track alone. It was rumored that some local horsemen wanted to pool their resources and rent the driving park from Pierce in March 1909. By April, Charles Atwood and Alex McLaren had stabled their horses, but there were absolutely no discussions of racing. The Rockford Amateur Driving Club believed that it could lease other land or build a new track for the future. The old qualms about the driving park, such as the difficulty getting to the grandstand and not being located near the streetcar line, were once again resurrected. Horses vanished from the track, and new automobiles and motorcycles took their place.

7

MOTORCYCLES TEAR UP THE TRACK

The Rockford High School track team ran tryouts at the driving park. On May 15, 1909, a track meet between the Rockford High School track team (Crimson) and the Freeport Pretzels was planned. Yet again, rains the day before made the track soggy, but it must not have bothered the Rockford team. They defeated Freeport 91–26. Two weeks later, Rockford hosted East Aurora. The Aurora team arrived in Rockford on the Chicago, Burlington and Quincy Railroad and were "confident of victory." Rockford coach Lloyd Heth put his confidence in Captain Brabrook, Woodward, Dowdakin, Hall, Wormwood and Frisbie. Aurora's feelings of victory proved correct, but not by much. They defeated the Rockford team 66–60. Apparently, the "dash men" could not run fast enough.

Hopes for auto racing began to spring up in June. Ben Fay came to Rockford to visit friends and family. He had been living in Los Angeles and had promoted racing there. It was hoped that he could arrange for an auto meet for July 4 at Rockford Driving Park. Nothing came of these hopes for July 4, but another meet was arranged for August 1 by another Ben—Ben Cope. The newly formed Rockford Motorcycle Club had twenty-five to thirty members who rode Indian, Davidson, Rex and Thor machines. They proposed sprint races, five-mile races and a ten-mile race. Some races were to have a "flying" start, while others had a "standing" start. Everything seemed excitingly perfect—except the date. For unknown reasons (probably due to weather or the desire for more entries), the races were postponed until August 15. That date did not pan out, either, as the track was "underwater." The riders planned for the next Sunday, August 22. The numerous delays only made the excitement intensify. The clubs' day of racing drew a crowd of three hundred people. Entry fees and a small gate fee were collected for Labor Day races. Approximately fifty automobile drivers became interested, and both groups met at the Nelson House. Challenges were barked out and ideas were developed, but no solid schedule was decided upon.

Nevertheless, the *Daily Register Gazette* cautioned against such races. The journalist claimed that Rockford's track was not built to accommodate automobiles or motorcycles, and it was too dangerous to race at such high speeds. The newspaper editorial expounded that the driving park track itself was sandy, and those 1904 automobiles had lower top speeds than current vehicles. Earlier in August, racers at the Indianapolis Motor Speedway had met their deaths behind the wheel for glory and adrenaline. The *Daily Register Gazette* article ended with, "One human life is worth more than all of the race meetings ever held or the pleasure which spectators can get out of them." The newspaper writer had a point.

The *Morning Star* reassured readers that no one would be killed at the Rockford track, and that there would be races on Labor Day: "There are few cars capable of speed sufficient to make much trouble and it is doubtful if the amateur drivers have sufficient nerve to put them to the limit on the turns and cause any trouble. The track is flat and hard and tires will travel smoothly with little opportunities for upset." The *Morning Star* continued to state that drivers that pushed their vehicles "to the limit" would race one at a time to avoid crashing. On September 4, the list of events was published in the *Daily Register Gazette*. Eight races were planned, but the number of entries was not listed.

Rockfordians had many options for how to spend their Labor Day. A parade was held in the morning. Harlem Park was open. Baseball games were held. The Orpheum Theater and Grand Opera House planned shows. There was a picnic for Old Settlers in Rood Park that began with a speech by Mayor Mark Jardine. A skating rink opened. Then, there were the races at Rockford Driving Park that began at 2:00 p.m. The *Daily Register Gazette*'s fears were in vain. The day's eight races proved to be a success for the fans (there were seven hundred in attendance) and profitable. Organizers planned to meet at the Nelson Hotel again. The *Morning Star* made it clear to its readers that auto racing was favored by Rockfordians because they chose to spend their day at the driving park and not stay away in fear of witnessing a tragedy at the track.

Another meet was planned for October 1, but it must not have panned out, because there were no reports of it in any of the newspapers. In the meantime, another auto club was beginning to take shape. It was to be formed over the winter and would hold official meetings and events in 1910. The Interurban Railway Company proposed to reconstruct the Huffman and Fulton rails to accommodate the driving park with its original rail line down Huffman Boulevard. This caused property values along the proposed route to soar. The newspapers cheered the decision, and the future for the driving park became bright again as many groups developed an interest in holding events there.

On January 7, 1910, the *Morning Star* reported the tale of Thomas Price. Price had been a resident of Rockford and around Rochelle for a time, then moved to Iowa and eventually returned to Winnebago County. He believed that he had made a deal with the T.J. and T.T. Burns brothers to lease their Burritt farm, so he moved back to the area. When he arrived, he was shocked that the Burns brothers had broken the agreement and remained in possession of their farm. This left Price and his family in limbo and in subzero temperatures for two weeks. All of his goods remained in train cars in the Milwaukee yards. Finally, Price hired lawyer B.A. Knight and leased the Rockford Driving Park until his case was settled. The case was heard in January but delayed because the Burns brothers lived in Burritt and had difficulty traveling to Rockford in the winter to defend themselves. The case was postponed. In February, the Burns brothers stated that they reneged on the deal because they believed that Price was "not a good farmer." Unfortunately for Price, the case must have dragged out and was finally officially dismissed four years later on December 23, 1914.

On February 18, 1910, a news story appeared concerning the driving park. Even Rockfordians were surprised at the announcement. An international aviation meet was under consideration to be held at the park. The Aero Club of Illinois (located in Chicago) considered Rockford as a possible site for the event because the members feared the potential of an airplane landing on "the Blackstone hotel or any other large Chicago building." Charles Lundberg, the president of the new Auto Club of Rockford, immediately dispatched a letter of invitation to the president of the Aero Club of Illinois. H.H. Havens and Everett Barnes could not wait to fly. At the end of February, they announced that they would attempt to fly their newly constructed plane either at the Willoughby Farm (located east of the driving park) or at the driving park. The Rockford Country Club offered its property for the exhibition, but Havens and Barnes declined, fearful that they would land on one of the golf course's bunkers.

Spring returned vitality and promise to the park. In March, horsemen gathered the capital needed and leased the driving park for training and potential races. There were thirty horses stabled for training. If there were to be any races, they would be organized around the Rockford Automobile Club dates. In April, the Rockford High School track team planned their school track meet, and the sophomore class of 1912 looked to have the most promise. The first meet for the Rockford team was against Rochelle. Despite the promising outlook, Rockford was defeated by Beloit and trounced by Sterling. School officials blamed the tough start on the lack of a school gymnasium. The team's last meet was in Aurora, and hopes were not high.

The summer was quickly approaching. No events for any type of racing were planned for the months of June, July or August. The Aurora racetrack held four days of racing during the summer, but the track later suffered from a terrible storm. Finally, in September, motorcycle races were proposed for the Rockford Driving Park. Initial reports stated that general admission was charged, and at least fifty machines were entered for three races (three-, five- and ten-mile races). Seven races were actually held; no one was injured, and the speeds were fast. The top performing brand of motorcycle that day was Excelsior, because that type of motorcycle placed either first or second in every race.

The park became quiet again. No more races of any sort were planned. At the end of October, a group of agricultural and city leaders came together at Memorial Hall to discuss a new agricultural association for a fair to be held in Winnebago County. Ideas for sites were floated, and once again, the driving park was proposed. Many new buildings and improvements were needed. The meeting closed without a decision. One motorcycle race meet and a few track meets were held that year. That was it. Yet again, no group had the ability to conduct regularly scheduled events.

On January 13, 1911, the *Daily Register Republic* reported that Iowa and Illinois endurance motorcycle riders from around the area would compete in July. In anticipation, motorcycle races were scheduled for the Rockford Driving Park for July 3 and 4. On February 3, it was reported that the Rockford Motorcycle Club met at 422 East State Street for a "smoker" and a meeting. In preparation for the year's races (which now included races for Memorial Day and Labor Day), one safety concern was taken into account. The track itself was a "flat track," because it lacked banked turns. Drivers and riders could lose control in the turns. It was proposed that the turns be banked six feet high and the grandstand be modified to handle the potential crowds. Indian, Thor and Excelsior motorcycle manufacturers would send representative riders to the meet to promote their products. The Federation of American Motorcyclists would ensure official times, rules and that all members could participate. Leisure motorcyclist members could ride in groups to different cities from Rockford on Sundays.

In March 1911, a "motordrome" was proposed to be built in the driving park. D.A. Kramer, from Freeport, promoted the building of a motordrome in Rockford because it was centrally located and near Chicago. His brother successfully ran a motordrome in Los Angeles. The project would cost $5,000, but Kramer would have pitched in $2,000 (to have control of the majority of the stock), so the Rockford Motorcycle Club would have to raise the remaining $3,000. More pressing than this new scheme was the need for new offices. The clubhouse at the driving park was too small for the club's fifty-four members. A banquet was held on March 16. While the motorcycle club seemed to be in a malaise, the Rockford High School boys' track team could not wait for another season.

Coach Lloyd Heth seemed positive. Many members of the team had already been spotted running around the driving park track before tryouts even occurred. Others bragged about their names appearing on the record board, but those records would not be broken at Rockford Driving Park. In April, it was announced by Coach Heth that the track meets would not be held at the driving park because the fairgrounds track was closer to the school. Another reason given was that the track at the fairgrounds was in better shape, "having a third of a mile cinder track and a hundred yard straightway." The *Republic* added that the crowds at the track meets would be bigger at the fairgrounds because they were located closer to downtown and the business districts.

A small article appeared in the April 11, 1911 *Morning Star*: "One of the spots for a fine subdivision is the old driving park. The land lays nice and could be reached by car service with little additional cost. It will not be long before this is broken into. Several real estate men have tried to put this deal over. The time will soon come, however, when it will be done." Subdivisions were being built south and west of the park. Of course, this became a reality, but not for another twenty years.

8

"TWENTY YEARS AGO..."

*T*he year 1911 was the twentieth anniversary of the opening of Rockford Driving Park. It was also the year that Rockford expanded its border northward across Auburn Street to include some of the neighborhoods south of the driving park. Rockford Driving Park was frequently mentioned in the newspapers throughout the entire year, but mostly in the "Twenty Years Ago" sections. Journalists recounted the glorious opening year, with all of its triumphs and setbacks, and the year 1911 filled with both for the track.

The Rockford Motorcycle Club wanted to move its offices out of the driving park but continued to lease the track. The club planned to hold its first racing meet on Decoration Day. There were absolutely no mentions of horses being trained or stabled there. Ed O'Connor advertised a "good serviceable horse for sale, cheap" in May. Even the Rockford High School track team no longer had their meets there, because the location was too far from their school. The Rockford Driving Park seemed to be abandoned again in April 1911—but not for long.

Rockford High School changed its mind about using Fairgrounds Park because the track there was not yet rolled or wide enough for nine to ten young men to run on. On May 20, a track meet between Rockford, East Aurora and Elgin High Schools was held at Rockford Driving Park. Approximately forty-one athletes competed, but not on time. The East Aurora team showed up late, so Elgin and Rockford began a race between their teams. Once the first races had been run, East Aurora arrived. The first races were considered practice races, and the three teams proceeded to compete as originally organized. Rockford won the meet by fourteen and a half points. Another meet was held between Freeport and Rockford just weeks later, again, at the driving park, because renovations to the fairgrounds' track were uncompleted.

The Rockford Motorcycle Club announced the program for Decoration Day races on May 27. The club planned to have seven races, including a novelty race between a motorcycle and an automobile. Spectators were transported from the streetcar line to the park by buses, admission was twenty-five cents and the Rockford Military Band provided entertainment between races. E.K. Barnes was appointed the referee, and Will Barnes's Ford raced against a motorcycle.

Approximately one thousand spectators enjoyed the Decoration Day races at driving park. Charles DeSalva broke a track record on an Indian motorcycle, gunning around the mile track in 1:02. DeSalva's time beat the previous track record set by Thomas L. Timmons by a single second. Elmer Friels won both of the single-cylinder events, but Willard Fiske from Beloit was the best rider of the day, having claimed two firsts and two seconds. The meet was a success, and the club prepared for a July 4 meet. According to the *Republic*, there were 225 motorcyclists in Rockford, and it anticipated that 100 would register for the July races. No mention was made of the outcome in the race between the motorcycle and the automobile.

Originally, the organizers of the Rockford Motorcycle Club had planned for seven races on July 4. That number was raised to ten. In addition to the races, an endurance race from Rockford to Dubuque, Iowa, was planned to begin on July 5. A banquet would honor the riders before they left, and if riders were capable, they could enjoy the Dubuque boat races on July 6. Excitement was in the air again for Rockford Driving Park, but then again, nothing was for certain. On July 4, the weather was extremely hot. Entries in the ten races were much fewer than expected, which made for sluggish performances. The only excitement was when A.G. Chapple from New York broke the track record by 3.5 seconds, so the new track record stood at 57.25 seconds per mile.

Meanwhile, horsemen became agitated. The township park commissioners acquired the Lathrop property along Fifteenth Avenue. The new Black Hawk Park was then surveyed. Horsemen wanted to plot a half-mile track on the grounds. The plat was located along the picturesque Rock River, and the hillside would provide natural seating for spectators. Vacant lots near the tract of land could be purchased, and new stables could be built. A new "gentlemen's driving club" could have organized training and amateur meets. The area inside of the track could be used as athletic fields. Access to the park would have been perfect, because it would only be one block away from the Fifteenth Avenue streetcar. Everyone would have benefited. Horsemen had demanded a new half-mile track for years. The commissioner of the park system did not deny the horsemen this request, and hopes of racing horses in Rockford blossomed anew. No horse racing returned to the driving park, and no plans were made for a new track at Black Hawk Park, either.

Horsemen became extremely frustrated and demanded a new scheme—this time near the driving park. Huffman Boulevard was proposed to become a horse "speedway," because it formed straightaways and simply needed to be properly paved. The Huffman Boulevard neighbors apparently did not object, and it was supposed that the park commissioners would not either. This plan went nowhere in a hurry, because there was room and a track just north of the boulevard—Rockford Driving Park, which was originally built for driving horses in 1890.

The Rockford Motorcycle Club decided to have one more meet before the end of the season. The club organized eight races, including a mile bicycle race, a five-mile automobile run and an exhibition by Billy Barnes's Mercer. To generate excitement, the club would decide a Winnebago County "champion racer."

The races were attended by one thousand people (the weather this time must have been perfect). There were thrills to be had in the races, too. Carl Bladstrom fell off his motorcycle, which loosened his handlebars at the start of a race. He quickly remounted his machine, made up the third of a mile behind the other riders and won his race. Clare Carratt rode against Bladstrom and only lost by the length of a wheel. During one of the other novelty races, riders rode one mile around the track, stopped and drank an entire soft drink, then remounted and finished the race. Despite crowning champions, the club decided to hold one more race meet at the beginning of October. The October meet was postponed due to weather, but once held, it, too, was successful, with three hundred spectators in attendance.

Winter approached. The park once again slumbered. In March 1912, the Rockford Motorcycle Club met in Bert Eastman's restaurant on East State Street. The members agreed that Rockford's population would buy more upgraded motorcycle models, mufflers would be closed while riding within city limits and that activities would surpass the previous year's, yet no solid plans were made for the upcoming year.

In April, the track saw its first action. Rockford High School held its school track meet there. Emory Hall was the new track team manager for Rockford High School, and Alfred Loos was their new coach. The two quickly secured a lease to host a triangular meet with West Aurora and Beloit High Schools at Driving Park. Tryouts for the final team were held at Fairgrounds Park. The Rockford team had to prove themselves, because they had yet to win any honors, and the other two schools already had done so. On the day of the meet, heavy rains deluged the track, and the meet was postponed a week. West Aurora could not accept the new date, because their schedule was too full. However, Freeport High School was contacted and agreed to take Aurora's place. Rockford was scheduled to compete against Freeport in Freeport, but Taylor's Driving Park, which had existed since the 1870s, was in the process of being torn apart. Without a home turf, Freeport gladly came to Rockford.

The weather cooperated. Rockford won decisively, followed by Beloit, then Freeport. A new pole vault record was set by Mackey of Rockford, and Homer Cotta of Rockford defeated Crouch of Beloit by only a few feet in the mile run. Rockford High School's other track meets were held against other schools in other towns, so the focus of the track returned to motorcycle racing. The first meet of 1912 was set for June 2, but not without controversy.

A "warning" advertisement was published in the *Daily Register Gazette* and the *Republic* the day before the races started. It claimed that the races would not be sanctioned by the Federation of American Motorcyclists. However, the other major newspapers published that the Federation of American Motorcyclists had wired approval for the meet on May 31. Carl Bladstrom was in charge of the meet, not the top officials of the club, such as Fred Sullivan, Clarence Carratt or C.H. Young. It seemed that the club had split. Advertisements that were in favor of the races stated that they were sponsored by the Rockford Motorcycle Club INC., not just the Rockford Motorcycle Club. On June 2, the official Rockford Motorcycle Club published another warning advertisement, calling the races "outlaw races," and warned that they were unsanctioned. Bladstrom assured a fast track, out-of-town riders (such as Chicago's "Motorcycle Mike") and records that would be broken.

Rain intervened. The races were postponed, and the "official" motorcycle club travelled to the Kishwaukee River for a day of fun and baseball (they originally had planned to go to Wisconsin, but the roads were unbearable). The following week also proved unfavorable for racing. This was not due to the weather, but because many of the riders had signed up for races in Beloit and in Milwaukee the following week. The "powers that be" were with the original Rockford Motorcycle Club.

Just like the *Titanic* that sank in 1912, so drowned the hopes of Rockford Driving Park. After the races were cancelled, Rockford Driving Park was reportedly going to be converted into a dairy farm in the fall. Julius Graham still owned the park and began plans to build a silo and dairy barn for his son-in-law Harry Needham. He planned to use new paper milk containers and have a dairy route. A bungalow was also built on the eighty-acre tract and is the only structure of the dairy farm that remains standing today. Lumber from the grandstand was used to construct the buildings. While inspecting the grounds for the new dairy farm, Graham noticed that lumber—and even sod in some places—was missing! William W. Winters was in the process of building a home south of the park and stole the lumber and sod. He carted away $50 of material and was held in the Winnebago County jail. Bond was set at $100. Winters promised to return the materials, and the charges of theft were dropped.

There was still the summer to race before any bovines stepped hoof into the park. July 4 races were announced on July 1. Indian and P.E.M. motorcycle manufacturers sent their top riders to Rockford. Prizes for the top three riders included motorcycle parts and gear, cigar boxes and fountain pens, and the winner of the five-mile Rockford Motorcycle Club members-only race would have his or her name inscribed on the "Cate" Cup. All of the prizes were put on display in the Smoke Shop's windows on State Street a week before the races. The grandstand was refurbished (ironically, since lumber from it was to be used for the building of the dairy farm) and could comfortably seat up to two thousand people.

Again, it rained, and it seemed like the drops fell only on the track, because the showers completely missed the city of Rockford. Two races were held before the rains made it too dangerous for racing to continue. Henry Olson found out how dangerous when his bike collided with Bert Johnson's during a practice run for the third race. Olson was badly bruised and cut and was sent to the hospital, but it was believed that he would recover quickly. The crowd had been large, considering all the other festivities in the city to celebrate the Fourth of July, but rain spoiled the fun. Thankfully, the national riders could stay in Rockford long enough for the races to be postponed. It rained again. In fact, the races were postponed a total of four times throughout the month of July. The club thought about offering a reward to discover who "hoodooed" or jinxed them.

On July 23, Albert Baker from Durand practiced with other riders on the track. When he attempted to pass another rider, his motorcycle went too far wide, got caught in the dust of the banked track edge and threw him to the ground. His goggle lenses shattered, and he got bruises and deep cuts on his face (he was lucky that his eyes were spared). The motorcycle he rode was also heavily damaged. The rest of the days' practices were safely run. Carl Swenson and Carl Bladstrom made quick work of the track and went around the mile in a minute flat. While waiting for the races to be held, the Rockford Motorcycle Club proposed to sponsor a 185-mile road race from Rockford into cities throughout Wisconsin and back to Rockford again. This, too, was cancelled due to rain. Finally, the Rockford Motorcycle Club gave up on Rockford and hosted races in Oregon, Illinois, that were a success. At least one thousand people attended, and fast times were recorded around their half-mile track. It seemed as if the summer season was quickly being washed away.

August 4 was a new hopeful day without rain. The races were finally run, and Bladstrom, Pehrson and Swenson ran an incredible ten-mile race, with Bladstrom racing to the finish line first. Since the month-late races were a hit, the club proposed the next races be held on August 24–25. Meanwhile, Julius Graham furiously paced in the courthouse, because the park had been included in a new Auburn Street sewer trunk line assessment. He angrily petitioned that the sewer did not service the park, so he should not have been assessed for it. The Rockford city attorney, A. Phillip Smith, believed that since the park's only outlet to the Rock River was the trunk line, Graham had no case. The assessment of the park was upheld in court.

Advertisements in newspapers read, "Don't Fail to See 'Shorty Matthews' on his 'White Streak.'" People in Rockford and around the area heeded this call. Near-record crowds came to witness the races held on August 24–25 (one thousand admission tickets were sold). The *Morning Star* was fearful of safety precautions but relaxed as it announced that local police would be on hand to keep crowds at a safe distance. Local businesses yet again provided prizes for the winners. Admission to the park was raised from the typical twenty-five cents to thirty-five cents, possibly due to the featured nationally recognized riders. The grandstand was free, and buses transported spectators from the streetcars to the gate for free as well. The admission was worth it. Matthews tore across the track and won seven races during the two-day meet. He set a new course mile record at 56.2 seconds (the previous record was one second longer). Three competitors had accidents. In the seventh race on day one, Willard Fiske hit the track's bank in the last turn and fell from his motorcycle. Only his finger was injured, but his motorcycle was totaled. Rudolph Thoms fell in the same turn but was uninjured. Michael Caffarella (also known as "Motorcycle Mike") fell from his motorcycle when his tire blew out, and he, too, was thankfully uninjured.

The Rockford Motorcycle Club was officially profitable. Attendance for the second day of races was between 2,000 and 2,500, so another meet was quickly arranged. On September 27, the club agreed to have a local-riders-only championship meet. The feature race was a twenty-five-mile race for a twenty-five-dollar purse. The admission was lowered to twenty-five cents, and the grandstand was free. The newspapers pressed spectators to come, because the park was to be converted into a dairy farm next season, so it would be their last chance to see motorcycle racing in the city. On the morning of September 27, the track was extra muddy. The races were cancelled and eventually run on October 6. Carl Bladstrom was crowned the county champion and won the twenty-five-mile race in twenty-six minutes. There were no reports of attendance or of profits for the club.

Harry Needham (Julius Graham's son-in-law) did not waste time. Only two weeks after the October 6 meet, he began to demolish the grandstand.

YOU SHOULD BECOME A MEMBER OF THE ROCKFORD MOTORCYCLE CLUB

The Rockford Motorcycle Club No. 55 of the Federation of American Motorcyclists extends a cordial invitation to all Motorcycle Riders not affiliated with this organization to become members this season.

You owe it to yourself to join this Club, for no other organization makes it a point to look after your welfare from a motorcycle standpoint. Your interest actively displayed will mean much to this Club. We need your help in initiating and promoting legislature which will benefit all motorcyclists and guard against the passage of laws and ordinances which will tend to infringe on our rights.

The time for you to enroll in this Club is now. If you are an old time motorcycle enthusiast or one of the 1913 crop we want you and your activity towards making this year the best and most enjoyable the motorcyclists of Rockford have ever known.

FRED W. SULLIVAN, Pres.   R. A. CROON, Sec.-Treas.
VIC. ANDERSON, Vice Pres   JOSEPH BICK, Rec. Sec.
FAY YOUNG, Capt.

The Rockford Motorcycle Club's newspaper advertisement encouraging people to join. *From Daily Register Gazette, March 22, 1913.*

The Henry and Edith Needham home. *Photograph by the author.*

The circular driveway that leads to the home is original, and wood from the grandstand was used to build it. *Photograph by the author.*

Arthur L. Johnson was also part of the Kiwanis Club that helped build Beyer Stadium, where the Rockford Peaches played. *From* Morning Star, *March 23, 1913.*

The grandstand was 210 feet in length and 40 feet in width. A crew of men tore down 40 feet of it but left the remaining grandstand intact. Needham intended to use the lumber to build a bungalow at the south end of the park. As for the track, Needham left it alone and decided to allow motorcyclists to use it for practice during the 1913 season. So much for the doom and gloom that the newspapers published about the track! But the Rockford Motorcycle Club had other ideas. The president of the club, Fred Sullivan, had talks with Riverside Park management about building a quarter-mile saucer track around the baseball field. Quarter-mile tracks were gaining in popularity, and they were more exciting than a mile track, but a month later, the club again returned to Julius Graham for another lease.

March was an exciting month for the motorcycle club. A motorcycle exhibition was organized at the club rooms at 302 East State Street (now C.J.'s Lounge on the northeast corner of State and Madison Streets). Motorcycle club advertisements, along with numerous motorcycle dealership advertisements, were published to entice more enthusiasts to join its ranks. On March 28, the club held a meeting; talks between Julius Graham and the club were sluggish, because Graham's lease price was high, but a compromise was slowly worked out. By April, the club had invested money into the structures at Rockford Driving Park. First, the grandstand was rebuilt to accommodate two thousand spectators. The track was widened for vehicles to travel between fifty-one and fifty-two miles per hour. Hill climbs, endurance races and race meets were announced. Proposals for the streetcar to run through Fulton to Rockton Avenue were also developed. Homes were built around the south end of Rockford Driving Park. Things were looking up.

9.

"START YOUR NATIONALLY RECOGNIZED ENGINES"

*T*he park was to be converted to a "scientific" dairy farm. There would be no more races. Yet, Andrew Gillette, a worker for Harry Needham, was seriously injured at the park while riding his motorcycle around the track. The park had been termed the "Old Driving Park" just as it was getting a new lease on life and gaining national attention. In mid-May 1913, the Rockford Motorcycle Club had complete control of the track and, with Julius Graham's permission, renamed the property "Rockford Motorcycle Speedway." The track was no longer for horse or for automobile racing but exclusively for the motorcycle club. However, high school track meets continued, and newspapers still frequently referred to the park as "Driving Park."

The club's first race meet was to be held on June 7 and 8 and featured nationally acclaimed riders. Excelsior Motorcycle riders Lee Humiston and Bob Perry signed contracts to appear in Rockford. On December 30, 1912, Humiston became the first rider to travel one hundred miles per hour on a mile board track in California. Not only would Humiston ride his motorcycle at the park, he also agreed to drive his 300 National Automobile around the track at high speed. Unfortunately, Humiston reneged on his Rockford appearance contract due to injuries suffered in an automobile accident shortly before the race meet. Perry's claim to fame was winning a three-hundred-mile grand prix race in Georgia, and he was considered to be a son to Ignaz Schwinn, who owned the Excelsior brand. Excitement built, and more than two thousand tickets were sold.

Conditions were perfect. Riders warmed up in the morning. Jack Woods, from Boston, had just finished racing down the home stretch in a practice run when the chain on his Eagle motorcycle broke. The wheel violently turned, and he was thrown through the south wire fence. Other riders who were practicing stopped to assist Woods. His chin and nose required three stitches, and he was badly bruised, but he wanted to race in the afternoon despite his injuries. His motorcycle was serviced at the Main Garage. "Motorcycle Mike" Caffarello had crashed his Indian motorcycle the previous day and was lucky to quickly get another motorcycle to race. The new machine was fast, because Caffarello completed a lap around the track in forty-six seconds. The enthusiasm was hard to contain.

Meanwhile, on June 4, the *Morning Star* reported on a motorcycle parade that was held downtown and led by the Rockford motorcycle police. Prizes were awarded to the best-decorated motorcycles. Jo Beck claimed first place with carnations on his machine and his young niece dressed as Cupid; she rode along in his sidecar and stole the hearts of admirers. Exel L. Anderson was witty and constructed a frame around his machine to resemble an airplane; as the breeze blew between the buildings, the propellers would spin. Hugo Anderson "dressed" his machine as an ostrich (legs and all), and Charles Ind created a battleship around his. The parade also served as an advertisement for the races that were to be held that weekend.

The track was in fine condition, for once, but the same could not be said of the motorcycles themselves. Many of the races were delayed due to broken chains or other various mechanical difficulties. The races were brisk and without accident until the last event. A bonus was promised to any rider who won the last event (which was fifteen miles in length) in under fourteen minutes. To secure his bonus, Motorcycle Mike Caffarella risked too much to achieve his goal. Apparently, Caffarella trailed Bob Perry in the last laps and took a turn too sharply. He was hurled into the air for some distance but was unharmed, because once he got back onto his feet, he tried to get back on his motorcycle as the engine was still running. Spectators, concerned for his well-being, ran out onto the track and flung their arms around him. He was later taken to the Rockford Hospital, where it was determined that he had no broken bones and was expected to race in the Sunday events. Perry not only won the race but also completed the fifteen miles in under fourteen minutes to claim the bonus.

Motorcycle Mike was not without drama on the following day, either. He was in first place in a ten-mile race but wanted to ensure that he kept the lead, because he knew Perry and other competitors were behind him. Unbeknownst to him, his competition was actually far behind. Caffarella gunned the engine around the northwest turn, but the machine began to waver. He once again lost control and landed hard on his left side. His Excelsior flipped twice in midair and landed on the track wall. Perry, who trailed behind, acted quickly to avoid the accident. Caffarella was lifted into an automobile and taken to the grandstand. Unbelievably, he wanted to participate in the next race despite being badly bruised and having a sprained ankle. His motorcycle was completely damaged, because the "front wheel had 'buckled' and the entire mechanism was damaged by the accident." Perry again became the star of the day and won many of the races.

One good turn deserves another. This time, it would be on four wheels instead of only two. Fred Sullivan, the president of the Rockford Motorcycle Club, arranged a deal between his club and Howard Smith in Chicago. Smith was a representative for nationally recognized riders and drivers. The only problem was the size of the track in Rockford. The turns were too tight for racing high-powered automobiles. It was agreed that the turns would be widened again as soon as possible. Louis Disbrow quickly signed a contract to appear in Rockford. Disbrow competed in the first four Indianapolis 500 races and in three American Grand Prix races. His "Jay-Eye-See" car was built by the J.I. Case Company at a cost of $18,000. Another driver who decided to appear in Rockford was Bill Endicott. Endicott was also a Case driver and came in fifth place in the Indianapolis 500 in 1912. Last, but not least, to appear was Joe Nikrent. Nikrent gained national fame when he won a 1909 road race from Phoenix to Los Angeles and raced in numerous Santa Barbara road races. It was believed that these drivers, along with others yet to be determined, would be in Rockford for several days to practice.

On June 21, Disbrow arrived in front of the *Rockford Morning Star* offices. A touring car had towed the Jay-Eye-See behind him. Small crowds gathered and clamored to experience the roar of the Jay-Eye-See engine. Disbrow obliged. Promptly, the rumble forced a policeman to arrive on the scene because he thought he heard the sound of a Gatling gun. Afterward, other national drivers arrived in Rockford and practiced on the track. One of the racers, Claude Newhouse, did not practice at all, because he did not want to show the other racers what he had.

The members of the Rockford Motorcycle Club knew this would be a big event. Officers from the Rockford Police Department dealt with crowd control. People from around the entire Northern Illinois region were expected to come. The drivers were also excited because the track conditions were perfect and the track modifications were complete. On June 22, the grandstand was filled with 3,800 to 4,000 spectators. People crowded along the park's wire fence, and 183 automobiles were parked in the infield and around the park. It was a day filled with good racing and two new broken records. Disbrow lowered the mile track record to 54.35 seconds. The coffers of the Rockford Motorcycle Club were replenished, and suddenly, the club gained national attention.

During the last weeks of July, Fred Sullivan attended a national motorcycle convention in Denver. He intended to entice nationally known motorcycle riders to come to Rockford to complete in a race meet on August 16–17. Sullivan used the profits from the professional auto races to attract riders and raised one race purse to $300. According to the *Daily Register Gazette*, Perry was unexperienced before the Rockford races and gained fame from them. In July, Perry defeated "Fearless" Charlie Balke, the dirt-track national champion. Perry remembered Rockford and quickly signed with Sullivan to reappear in Rockford while in Denver. Other riders who signed included L.S. Taylor, E.G. Baker, Harold Cole, Ray Comstock, Jack Wood and Fairbury, Illinois brothers Carl F. and William Goudy. Rockford riders Carl Swanson and Henry Pehrson were worthy of riding with the national professionals.

Spectators paid an expensive fifty-cent gate fee, but the grandstand and parking were free. Riders began to arrive in Rockford on August 15. Charlie Balke faced a rematch against Perry in Rockford. In fact, H.N. Kirk, the sales manager for Thor motorcycles, stated in the *Republic* that he had never seen so many professional riders at an event. The crowd was not disappointed. In the first race, Perry crashed his motorcycle. He was able to walk away and race again later. Carl Swanson finished second in front of his hometown throng. William Goudy and Balke locked handlebars for a moment (locking handlebars was a common trick) and then became separated. Perry trailed them. When Goudy and Balke slowed down to unlock their handlebars, Perry was forced to the outside and ran into the rough dirt. He lost control and flew off of his motorcycle into the barbed wire fence. Yet again, Perry was lucky in that he only sustained minor injuries. Carl Goudy won the heat. Perry got back on his machine and came in second in the second heat. The races continued on the next day. Neither Balke nor Perry was the "Man of the Day," as Carl Goudy won three out of the nine events on the first day.

On August 17, the last day of racing, there were numerous injuries and a new track record. In the first race of the day, Lee Taylor (who was the champion of Ohio) rounded the first curve of the track too tightly and lost control. He was forcefully thrown against a track fence but was uninjured. "Bugs" Leslie Allen was right behind Taylor and could not avoid hitting Taylor's machine. Allen was thrust off of his Excelsior and fell head-first into the dirt track. The audience gasped as Dr. W.P. Burdick rushed in his automobile to Allen's side. Allen was severely cut from his right eye to the back of his head. He had numerous other cuts to his abdomen and his legs. He was taken to the hospital tent and then to his room at the East Side Inn. A full recovery was expected, because there were no signs of internal injury. E.G. Baker skidded in the fourth race and received a third-degree burn on his left thigh. In the sixth event, Leo Bickenback lost control of his machine and severely burned his back in the process. It was feared that he had internal injuries, but he left town before any doctor could thoroughly examine him. However, Perry and Balke were in top form.

In every race in which they competed against each other, Balke beat Perry. Balke fearlessly took the turns wide, dangerously kicking up clouds of dust to win. Balke even lowered Perry's Rockford track record to 52.5 seconds. Perry, if he was not racing against Balke, took first place against his other rivals and walked away with $200 in prize money. Perry said, "Balke is the cleanest little fellow I ever rode against. I'd rather beat him than anybody else, for when you've beaten him, you've done something." The Rockford Cycle Company wasted no time advertising Excelsior motorcycles as winning motorcycles. Rockford benefited economically again as hotels, motorcycle shops, mechanics, restaurants, the streetcar railway and—last but not least—the Rockford Motorcycle Club made lots of money that weekend.

The Rockford Driving Park or "Motorcycle Speedway" became dormant again in October. The Rockford Motorcycle Club hosted road trips and a dance at Germania Hall instead. In November, it was agreed that the club would show some motorcycles at the annual Coliseum car show. By 1915, the high school no longer held track meets at the park because it had its own track. The *Morning Star* practically declared that horse racing was "in the graveyard." Motorcycle manufacturers decided to not build any more racing machines, so the *Morning Star* believed that no more motorcycle races would be held at the park in the new year—the paper's writers were correct. Another reason behind the absence of motorcycle racing was due to the streetcar company not being able to provide service to the park. People simply did not want to walk that many blocks from the Main Street line to the park. The company had promised a return of service, but no action was taken. In May, Rockford-area golfers believed that the park could hold a nine-hole golf course. Money was agreed to be paid, but no action took place. The prime time of summer waned away. Even Henry Needham, the son-in-law of park owner Julius Graham, must have had a rough summer. He placed a newspaper advertisement for his McCormick binder that had cut less than one hundred acres. It was not until August that an event for the park was declared. The Rockford Motor Club (which changed its name from the Rockford Automobile Club in 1912 to broaden its membership) decided to hold its annual Kennedy Hill Climb on August 7 and a meet in the park on August 14–15. The Rockford Motor Club had the largest membership numbers (471) in Illinois outside of Chicago. The meet was to be for amateurs and for members of the club only, so AAA official sanctions were unnecessary.

For some unknown reason, the hill climb and the races were postponed. The hill climb was held on August 18—a Wednesday, curiously enough—and the races were not to be held until September. The hill climb proved to be very successful, because records were broken in all of the events except one, and many trophies and cash prizes were awarded. September came, and no races were held in the park. The newspapers made no comment as to why. The Rockford Motor Club could have had the same concern as the motorcycle club in regard to transportation for spectators or weather issues, or perhaps the club was focused on the building of the new clubhouse.

One of the remedies for the park's dismal situation was yet again proposed by the manager of the streetcar company in March 1916. The new plans for his company proposed sixty-four new blocks of track, the removal of old loops and transportation from interurban cars to streetcars. Improvements would cost the company around $400,000. The Rockford Motorcycle Club met in the spring, too, to discuss the calendar of events, which included plans for a race meet to be held at the driving park—yet more promises, promises. Henry Needham, in the meantime, used the park as his private playground for guests at his home within the park grounds. The Rockford Overland Bowling Team came to the grounds for a banquet, then competed in athletic events on the track. Needham gave an exhibition of "hitting flies."

By August, the Rockford Motorcycle Club may have turned plans for a race meet into an actuality. On August 19–20, a motorcycle race meet was held for professional riders only. Professional motorcycle racer Bob Perry was the first to sign up for the contest (he later withdrew), and Don Johns (Oakland, California) and Morty Graves (Springfield, Massachusetts) signed up afterward. Johns was a "born racer," since he grew up across the street from an Indian motorcycle dealership in Los Angeles. When he was a kid, the men in the shop would allow the youngster to learn all about the machines that they worked on. At age twelve, he prepared for his first race but discovered that racing regulations stated that he was too young. Instead, he stood along the sidelines and watched Charles Balke win. Johns simply had to wait for his time. In 1911, he broke numerous nationally held records and was considered a national breakout star. In 1914, in Dodge City, Kansas, after he set another speed record, the crowd surrounded his motorcycle and pulled souvenirs off of it.

Graves began his career in 1906, when motorcycles were mostly wooden bike frames and rims. As the years progressed, he developed a name for himself and lost a three-hundred-mile race in the last mile when he ran out of gas. Graves retired at the end of 1915 at the tender age of twenty-five but somehow committed himself to the Rockford event in 1916.

Other riders who signed up were Glenn Stokes and Fred Luther for Excelsior; Maldwyn Jones for Merkle; Ray Creviston for Indian; and Otto Walker, Ray Weishaar, Irving Janke and Leslie "Red" Parkhurst for Harley-Davidson. All of these riders were nationally known and held contracts for the manufacturers' teams. Stokes won a ten-mile race in Chicago in May. Jones was considered the best dirt-track racer in the Midwest who had the best and worst luck. He won many races but lost many, too, due to mechanical errors in the final laps. He also designed an improved racing helmet with a cork lining to absorb the impact of an accident. Creviston was a tough-talking rider from Indiana who was quickly became Indian's greatest rider. Walker was the first Harley-Davidson rider to win a national race for the company, and he beat Graves when he ran out of gas in 1915. Wieshaar won the 1916 one-hundred-mile race in Detroit just before the race event in Rockford. Parkhurst drove delivery vehicles for his father's business despite being constantly ticketed for speeding. He became a member of the first Harley-Davidson racing team and won an event in 1916 in front of a crowd of eighteen thousand spectators in New York.

The Rockford Motor Club charged thirty-five cents for advance tickets from downtown garages and cigar stores and charged fifty cents at the gate. A truck carried spectators from Ashton's corner at State and Main Streets, and the streetcar company transported passengers from the streetcars to the park by bus. A bicycle race was promoted as well, featuring Luigi Norelia, a popular Belgian racer. On Saturday, there were five-, ten-, fifteen- and twenty-five-mile races and one race to beat the track record. On Sunday, there were only three events: five-, ten- and one-hundred-mile races. People from Freeport, Belvidere and Rockford bought tickets en masse, the track was in great condition (Henry Needham was in charge of a small army of graders) and everything was set. No disappointment this time, either.

No reports of the winners were made in the newspapers except for the one-hundred-mile race on Sunday. Creviston was not thought to make the Rockford race meet due to other commitments. When his motorcycle arrived at the Rockford Motorcycle Club, members were thrilled, because he had just won a one-hundred-mile race in Galesburg. In Rockford, Creviston led the entire race until lap eight-seven, when he made a pit stop and Weishaar passed him. When Creviston returned to the track, he thundered around the track in forty-eight seconds to catch and surpass Weishaar. Not only did he win the one-hundred-mile race on Sunday, he also set a new one-hundred-mile race national record and a new track record of forty-eight seconds per lap. Weishaar finished second, followed by Stokes and Janke. A huge number of people (3,500) came to witness the dirt-flying machines.

The Rockford Motorcycle Club collected enough money on Saturday to offset its expenses, so Sunday's revenues became pure profit. The successful motorcycle races led to the Rockford Motor Club announcing weeks later that another race event for local automobile drivers would be held in September. Ira Bell, owner of the Rockford Overland Company and member of the Motor Club, took care of the entries. He was also the head of the Overland bowling team and influenced the Rockford Bowling Association to sponsor the races. In the evening, after the races were over and the spectators were all gone, a pair of couples raced their own machines on the track. Deputy Sherriff Baldwin was called to remove them. They were informed that the track was private property and warned against future excursions. Henry Needham refused to press trespassing charges; he did not want to appear in court.

Drivers from Freeport and Beloit entered the races that were held on September 17. The Rockford drivers included Parley "Packey" McFarland (Buick Special), Joe Johnson (Marmon), Ralph "Speedy" Wilson (Ford Special), Whitey Bergstrom (Know Special), Gene Hall (Cadillac) and F. Taylor (Marion). Many drivers practiced on the track for weeks before the event. Admission was fifty cents, but parking was free. A crowd of between 1,500 and 2,000 people ventured to the park to see the events. Vern Abbott of Woodstock won the twenty-five-mile race (Johnson placed fourth, and Wilson placed fifth), and McFarland won the fifty-mile race. Abbott averaged fifty-three miles per hour, and McFarland averaged forty-nine (probably because his car and the cars he raced against were larger). Both races were run without accident; only numerous mechanical problems with bearings and oil leaks were encountered. In the fifty-mile race, Hall's Cadillac had to be pushed across the line due to a burned bearing. Another competitor's car was removed from the track when it completely stalled and could not be restarted after lap fifteen. The day was a good one, and the Rockford Bowling Association made a profit.

The Rockford Motorcycle and Motor Clubs stated that since their events in late 1916 were a success, they each planned to have at least two events in 1917. The Needhams proposed to demolish the old wooden grandstand completely and replace it with a concrete structure. However, world events in Europe dashed all of those hopes. The newspapers chronicled troop movements and the militarization of the United States throughout 1916.

10.

DALY CHANGING FORTUNES

Despite President Woodrow Wilson's call for Americans to remain "neutral in mind and in deed," most manufacturers of motorcycles and automobiles already thought of national defense contracts. This meant that manufacturers would no longer pay for race teams (or displays, meets and such that attracted civilian populations to purchase their products) or develop racing machines. War also meant that resources such as gasoline and rubber were rationed. It was undetermined when professional riders and drivers would again appear in the driving park, if ever. Locals would have to fill the gap.

On April 14, 1917, during the same month that the United States declared war against the Central Powers in Europe, Carl Bladstrom, who owned an Indian dealership, proposed a twenty-four-hour motorcycle record race in Rockford Driving Park. The idea was to ride as many miles as possible in a twenty-four-hour period, and according to the *Republic*, it was a national phenomenon. The date of the race was set for Decoration (Memorial) Day, and four riders supposedly entered. If the race occurred, none of the Rockford newspapers reported on it, and that's why it is doubtful that it ever happened.

During the summer of 1917, the Great War directly affected the driving park. Henry Stainthorpe Needham answered Uncle Sam's call. Needham became part of the YMCA War Work Council in Chicago. According to his World War I draft card, he was employed in "recreation near overseas work." While Needham completed his patriotic duties in Chicago, his wife,

Edith, and his daughter, Catherine, moved out of the driving park bungalow and in with Edith's parents (Julius and Emily Graham). The Needhams tried to sell "for cheap" two of their ponies, a Studebaker basket buggy, a saddle and a harness. By November, Andrew J. Gilbert had taken over the Needham home and raised crops in the infield. Gilbert may or may not have been joined by newlyweds Albert E. and Lillian (Isaac) Hilton in the spring of 1918. Hilton sold silos in Pecatonica, married Lillian Isaac from Rockford, then moved into the driving park home and continued to farm on the dairy there throughout the war years.

After the war, the Needhams lived with the Grahams at 428 Kent Street (the home was built by Julius and still stands in front of the Tinker Swiss Cottage parking lot) until the mid-1920s. The Needhams never returned to the driving park home. In the 1920 U.S. census records, Needham operated a bowling alley. This made sense, because he was friends with Ira Bell, who was a director of the Rockford Bowling Association.

By World War I, most of the horse-training and driving personalities from the park's glory days had either moved on or died. However, one former personality, C.J. Franks, became directly involved in the war effort—but not in Rockford. Franks was a horse trainer and once controlled the driving park with B.C. Kimlin in the 1890s. In 1917, he was fully employed by the U.S. government to purchase horses in Roswell, New Mexico. Apparently, many people from the north-central Illinois area moved to that territory and became cozy neighbors.

In August and September 1916, the roaring engines of professional motorcycle riders and local racing automobiles could be heard for miles. The Great War stalled the park's potential. Instead, it became a sleepy dairy farm. Once the war was over, in February 1919, Charles Lee Daly of Minnesota leased the park from Julius Graham for three years.

Daly moved himself into the driving park house and his large amount of livestock onto the driving park grounds. He had had a considerable amount of success in the newspaper business and previous county fair organization experience. Daly began plans to improve the dormant track and dilapidated conditions or lack of fence around the park. Daly discussed reviving race meets and renewed interest in hosting the county fair at the park. At a meeting held at the Forest City National Bank, he proposed to plant the forty-acre infield with wheat that would be harvested in July. The empty field would then be used for farm implement displays and parking. Daly also proposed the construction of a few small buildings where women could display their talents, a temporary grandstand for viewing events and tents for other exhibits. For almost thirty years, since the driving park investors had searched for a site to build in 1890, the driving park was considered as a new location for the Winnebago County Fair. The fair had not been held for seventeen years. On April 8, 1919, the Rock River Fair Association officially received its incorporation papers from the State of Illinois. Its investments totaled $10,000, and the fair would undoubtedly be held on the driving park grounds. Daly was the key incorporator of the Rock River Fair Association, along with Fred C. Lange and Edward D. Hayes. As with Dr. H.L. McClellan in 1898, it took an outsider to breathe new life into the "dead asleep" park.

Men slowly returned from the fighting in Europe, and a county fair would be a pleasant experience for them. Construction began at once. A new, ten-thousand-seat

Photograph of Charles Lee Daly taken from *The City of Rockford and Her Men of Affairs*, which was written by Daly. *From Charles Lee Daly,* The City of Rockford and Her Men of Affairs, *New Illinois Stationery Company, 1920, 104.*

grandstand was to be built (Needham had used lumber from the old one to build his home on the driving park grounds). Hearty premiums for livestock and farm produce were offered in the amount of $10,000. However, the best element of the proposed fair, which was scheduled for August 26–29, was the return of what the driving park was originally built for: horse racing. Purses for races were set between $400 and $500. As early as April, new, electrically lit stables with one hundred stalls were built as horses once again trained in the park. By May and June, there were 111 horses registered for the fair's horse races.

Newspapers reported that an old, familiar character returned, too. The *Republic* exclaimed, "Fay Carney is coming back!" Carney, a one-time director of the driving park, entered his mare Alma Aquillin in the 2:14 trot. Carney's son Mike also entered. Carney had bought the horse from Dr. P.L. Markley (who was also a past driving park president) and was glad to race again for the first time in eight years. Another former Rockford Driving Park Association member returned, as T.D. Reber's son had a horse entered in a saddle class. Reber's heart swelled with pride. Even a *Daily Register Gazette* journalist couldn't believe his eyes. He had recorded the "glory days" of the driving park and remarked that many faces from the early days of the 1890s were gone, but some remained and reappeared in their former places. Fred Keyt, Elisha Thayer and Will Bennett were training or watching the next generation. The journalist eloquently remarked, "Recollections of the olden days brought tears to the eyes of many old-timers at the fair yesterday and made them realize that time is indeed swift in its flight. The long froth counter under the grand stand and the big wheel where the attendants used to shout 'The lucky star wins,' were things of the past and not in evidence yesterday." The old stable and barn were gone, but the "kite-shaped" mile track was the same in 1919 as it had been in 1890.

Letters were sent to farm implement manufacturers and to farmers. The letters explained the many reasons why the fair should be attended. The letter stated:

> *There are many reasons why you should show at Rockford. We have a drawing population of over 380,000 in a radius of thirty miles, fifty-six towns and villages. There are three hundred factories with a pay roll of $60,000 daily. There are five railroads and three interurban lines and we have beautiful Camp Grant training over 35,000 men for the new national army. More money changes hands daily in Rockford than in any city of its size in the northwest.*

Again, the park would economically benefit the Rockford community. Daly was a very motivated promoter. On May 9, at a community party given by the WCTU, he gave a speech pertaining to the new fair plans as well as expounding on the previous reasons to attend. His efforts quickly paid off, as over half of the area available for the farm machinery exposition was vouched for. Hundreds of concession vendors rented space. Churches began to build dining halls to raise money. Contractors steadily built a new grandstand, and a heavy barbed-wire park border fence was established. Pressure mounted not only for finishing the fair but for auto races.

Daly attracted nationally recognized automobile drivers to compete at the driving park, and advanced tickets sold once more. Large driver portraits were placed in the newspapers leading up to the event. Automobile dirt-track champion Sig Haugdahl, John Duray and Verne Soules all arrived in Rockford on August 1. Haugdahl drove his "big Italian Fist" Fiat car, Duray was in his Case and Soules drove his Darracq (a type of French-made automobile). Haugdahl's and Soules's cars were parked in local garages under sheets to protect them from the elements and prying eyes.

Meanwhile, Duray drove to the baseball park to watch Rockford's team beat Terre Haute. The sight caused much conversation and excitement. Fred Horey, the former champion, traveled to Rockford to take back his title from Haugdahl. Others were on their way, along with the Pacific Coast and All-American Auto Polo Teams; for each automobile, the driver would drive and the passenger would swing the mallet.

People from Chicago would soon have a chance to see the excitement. James McCartney and Fred Schlagel formed a new airline passenger company with service from Chicago to Rockford. Fares for flights were to be determined. Pilot Trent Frye flew from Ashburn Park in Chicago to Rockford in a Curtiss JN4D two-passenger (former) military plane and landed in Rockford Driving Park to prove it could be done. Frye had previous experience flying airplanes during the war and also as an aerial mail service carrier in Cleveland, Ohio. The driving park would serve as a base of operations. Captain Alex McCleod of Camp Grant claimed that Rockford needed an airfield and could be a critical stop for people just west of Chicago. The driving park was a suitable place because it was flat and near the city limits. All that was needed was a cement cross to mark the landing field for pilots. McCartney, most likely in an effort to increase interest, challenged Sig Haugdahl to a race against his newly arrived plane. The challenge was accepted and would be held on the August 6 race day. Every mode of transportation—planes, trains, horses, bicycles and automobiles—could now be found at the park. However, not everyone was pleased with the idea of a park airfield.

A *Republic* journalist reported that a chicken farmer near the park was distressed. His chickens were deathly afraid of airplanes because they thought that they were hawks. They ran around and sought safety against the "giant hawks." The journalist also claimed that the farmer's chickens were slowly starving because their heads were always cocked with one eye to the sky. The chickens lost weight and could be less profitable to the farmer. Residents near the driving park were distracted by automobiles roaring at a new track speed of seventy miles per hour.

Local officials acted as judges for the contest. An ambulance from the Red Cross was sent to the park in case of any accidents or spectator needs. Twenty special police provided crowd control. Jitney buses transported passengers from the streetcars to the park. Even nature helped out, as rain fell before the races started and drenched the track just enough to keep the dust down, which saved on sprinkling wagon expenses.

Spectators arrived by the thousands and paid fifty-cent entrance fees. Before the first race got underway, nature continued "sprinkling the track."

The winds picked up, and a section of grandstand canvas collapsed feet away from seated spectators. Thankfully, there were very few in that area, and no one was seriously hurt. The remainder of the canvas was removed, and the races started on time. The first race was won by Soules on a very sloppy track. The second race was named "the Camp Grant Sweepstakes" and could only be won by winning the best out of numerous heats. Duray won the first, and Haugdaul won the second. The heat only lasted a little under seven minutes. Continuing rains made it unsuitable to race, but conditions were still acceptable for automobile polo. The infield became a "playing field." Two ten-minute halves and a one-minute intermission were set for the game. At halftime, the game between the Pacific and All-American teams was tied at two goals. Spectators were thrilled by head-on collisions, overturned vehicles and locked wheels. By the end of the second half, the All-American team had pulled in front of the Pacific team, and they won by a score of 4–3. Afterward, the crowds began to filter out due to the pouring rains. The professional racers left the city for other races, and the proposed exciting races were cancelled. However, spectators were not disappointed.

Attention swung toward the next upcoming event—the county agricultural fair. Director Charles Daly was wise. Weeks before the fair, he hired groups of women to canvas the city to sell reduced-priced fair season tickets. Soldiers in uniform, children and city pioneers were admitted for free on opening day. Daly hired the Rockford Electric Company to electrify the park so that attendees could enjoy the fair at night. Various displays and entertainments were organized. He booked a Great War reenactment show (with pyrotechnics) entitled "Battle of the North Sea" to perform in the evenings. Captain D.P. Murphy was in charge of two captured German tanks and a vast group of large German guns (including a shell from the famed German one-hundred-mile gun "Big Bertha," one of only four known to exist in the United States at the time) on display by the Camp Grant recruiting officers. New models of tractors and automobiles could also be seen at the fair. On average, the tractor displays took up two hundred feet of display space. Many horses were expected to trot and pace in three races every day, including a one-horse gimmick show. Don Alimo was a famous pacing horse because he would line up at the starting line and, without rider or driver, would pace entirely around the track to return to the barn. Saddle classes were for mostly Rockford riders. Exhibits were on the road and on the way to the park. One, in particular, was from the Red Cross.

The Red Cross planned to have two large tents on the grounds for the entire fair. One tent was for first aid and located at the front gate, but it also served in another way. Nurses, when not concerned with spectator emergencies, taught the public proper childcare safety. The second tent displayed items created by appreciative Russian schoolchildren for work provided in Russia after the Great War. The Red Cross also exhibited care items sent to sailors and soldiers during the Great War in addition to knitted items for Belgian refugees. Not ones to miss out on a fundraising opportunity, the ladies of the Red Cross sold lunch items, as well. A lot of coordination was required, but the task of organizing the modern 1919 fair was completed. Across town, at the new Blackhawk Park, other preparations took place.

A new Rockford Zoo developed during the time of the fair but was not yet completed. The Ringling Bros. Circus donated an elephant named Babe, but it had arrived in Rockford without a place to stay. A shed was specially made to serve as its home. When Charles Daly first met Babe, the elephant blew dust at him. Daly brought Babe to the fair to act as a family attraction. While she was tethered, people who walked by her were given a bag of freshly roasted peanuts. They were then asked to give a small donation to the Children's Home in return.

Crowds numbering around fifty thousand were expected, and they came. The Hess and Hopkins, Emerson-Brantingham, Ingersoll and Barber-Colman factories closed. The fair opened to such large crowds that they unsuccessfully clamored for the fair to remain open an extra day. Fair attendees always had something to do. They ate at concession stands, watched acrobats, stayed for vaudeville shows and listened to live music and "red-headed comedians" (The Vans) while seated in the grandstand. Livestock shows, home economic exhibits, numerous industrial and organizational exhibits and, of course, Babe were all on display.

Horse racing returned. A "jockeyed" horse race was run for male and female riders. Martha Colman of Rockford won, and an eleven-year old girl from Pecatonica, Viola Palmer, came in second in the ladies' race. Palmer rode without a saddle or crop, and in a practice race on Sunday before the fair opened, Midnight jumped over the track fence and had thrown Palmer. No problem. She just got back on. C. Herbert Lewis (a portly jockey who weighed two hundred pounds) won the gentleman's race on Maid Marion.

On the second day, horse racing of the harness variety returned to the park. The grandstand and all available places to witness the races were taken. Thousands of spectators were estimated to be in attendance, and they were in for a good show. There were accidents in two races. Matt Trask was a seventy-three-year-old Civil War veteran, former gold prospector and horse-racing driver. In the third heat of the first race, he fell out of his seat in the home stretch. He was trying to maneuver between horses and got too close to the bank of the inside of the track. Thankfully, neither he nor his horse was injured. William H broke, reared and became entangled in his harness, which resulted in the driver being thrown to the side of the track. Alongside the reports of the horse races, numerous livestock and home economics competition winners were listed in the newspapers. Even Charles Daly entered mallard ducks and won a premium.

The Rockford Driving Park had never been so successful or profitable since its opening days. The final estimated crowd totaled just below fifty thousand. The Rock River Fair Association began work on the 1920 fair. The first issue up for debate was its location. A majority of the fair association members wanted to purchase land and not suspend the driving park lease. Julius Graham believed that the driving park's eighty acres were worth $1,000 an acre. Suitable land for a fair was offered near West State Street for $600 an acre. Daly would have to develop other events to make Rockford Driving Park an entertainment destination if the plan to move was approved.

In September, Daly traveled to Beloit, Elkhorn and Jefferson, Wisconsin, to "line up" some horses to arrange a late fall meet. He believed owners and trainers would be interested in one more pace or trot around the track before the winter snows. Several dates were given. Daly wanted to make sure area horsemen were available and may have wanted to stable horses at the park once all of the local fairs ended. His efforts did not go unrewarded. The dates were set for Friday, October 3, and Saturday, October 4. Racing would begin at three o'clock in the afternoon. Horses from Rockford, Belvidere and Beloit stabled at the driving park. George Sumner and William Mahon from Pecatonica owned a horse that paced a fast 2.05-minute mile. He was so fast that during the meet, he would not be raced against any other local horses, only against time itself. Daly even sought horses and jockeys for nondriving races. The track was listed in good condition, so Daly did not stop with just horses. Entry slips for a later amateur automobile race meet were presented to local drivers as well. A race meet for automobiles and motorcycles was planned for October, right after the horse races. Daly must have been constantly at work to promote the driving park—he was just the sort of person the track needed.

Thirty horses were entered for the race meet. There were three races a day over the course of the two-day meet. However, when Daly and the rest of Rockford woke up on Friday morning, they listened to raindrops hitting their roofs. The *Daily Register Gazette* headlined the postponement on the front page. No matter. The races would have to wait until Saturday. In the meantime, the track was dragged and rolled. Perhaps more people could come to witness the races on the weekend anyway.

On Saturday, drizzle again threatened to cancel the races. Officials conferred and decided that the track would be heavy but good enough for races. Spectators walked to the grandstand, but not in droves. Only seven hundred came, which was well short of the one thousand Daly thought he would have. The races were not exciting, either, because horses won in straight heats. The only notable news item from the meet was an accident that involved Matt Trask—the same Matt Trask who had an accident during the fair. This time, the harness on Trask's horse broke, which sent him backward and off his sulky seat again. Since he trailed at the time, he was not involved in a more serious accident. The races planned for Sunday were called off due to rain. Daly had to have been disappointed, but he had automobiles and motorcycles to think about for the next weekend.

Drivers and riders practiced the week before the motorized races. One motorcyclist wanted to win Daly's special new track record cash prize. While in a turn, he let the throttle out completely. The result landed him on his backside in the infield while his machine continued on at top speed and crashed into the outside rail. The rider was not identified to the journalist, but apparently, he had lost his nerve and arranged for a substitute rider on the day of the race meet. Three automobile races and three motorcycle races were to be held on October 12.

On the morning of the races, things did not begin so well. Nicholas Frendahl of Beloit, along with his mechanic Dr. Fred Kostlevy (a dentist) by his side, practiced laps around the track. Frendahl came out of a turn and lost control of his vehicle. Several spectators stood near the fence as the car began to wobble and zigzag. Spectators scrambled as the automobile crashed through an infield wire fence and threw Kostlevy several feet out of the vehicle. According to the *Daily Register Gazette*, it was determined that he did not break any bones, but he complained of abdominal pain. However, the *Republic* claimed that he fractured his left arm. Internal injuries were feared, but after a night in the hospital, Kostlevy began to recover. Meanwhile, Frendahl was uninjured because he remained in the vehicle. The cause of the crash was not speed but mechanical steering issues. The wreckage was cleared, and races began.

There were an estimated two thousand spectators there to witness the motorized sport that Sunday afternoon. The races were filled with tire

Above: Laurens Lander in his automobile in an unknown location. *Courtesy of Truman Lander.*

Right: The starting line and the judges' stand. Laurens Lander and his rider Lloyd Worden are in the car with headlights. *Courtesy of Truman Lander.*

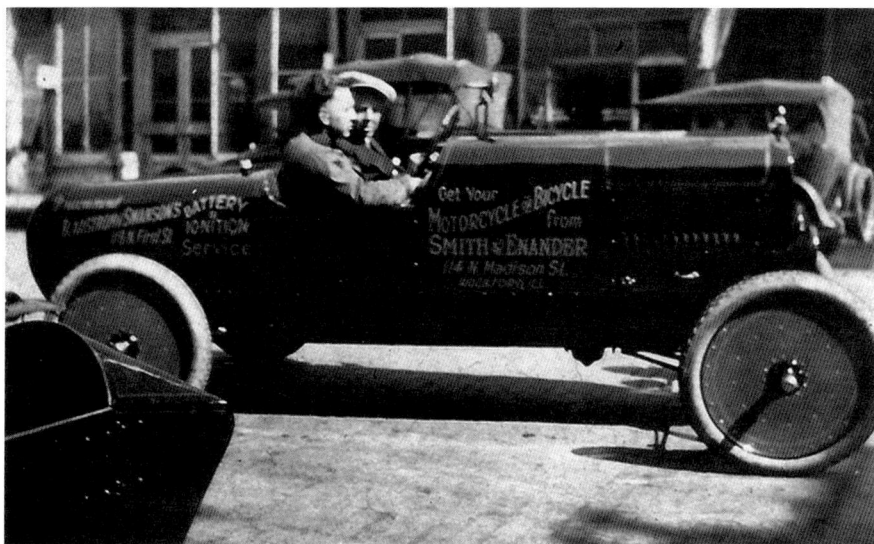

Smith and Enander opened a sales and repair shop at 114 North Madison Street. Smith was a regular rider at Rockford Driving Park. *Courtesy of Michael DeBock.*

changes and leader changes, but no accidents. Howard Ryan from Rockford won the twenty-five-mile motorcycle race on a Harley-Davidson, but Claude Smith, who resided at Camp Grant and rode an Indian, pushed him all the way to the end and finished second only yards behind. The Fred O. and Fred H. Eddy team of Beloit won the automobile races, since Frank Carmack needed to change a tire in the last laps.

The success quickly made Daly announce another race meet for November 2. All of the racers were welcomed back to retain their honors or to win them. All of the entrants agreed to race no matter what weather occurred that day. Motorcyclists Claude Smith and Howard Ryan developed a sizable bet, according to off-record sources.

The newspapers touted the rivalries between the Eddys, Carmack, Smith and Ryan, but the day was taken by Charlie Spataford. Spataford drove so fast that he literally sped a mile a minute. He appeared to be a clear winner for the twenty-five-mile race until his rear axle broke. No problem. He managed to pull his automobile into the pit area, replaced the broken axle with one from fellow racer Joe Jackson and continued to race. Andrew Rotello won the five-mile automobile race, Frendahl won the ten-mile race and Smith won all three of the races. Carmack was not only a driver but also a member of the 872 Aero Squadron. He asked Daly if he could

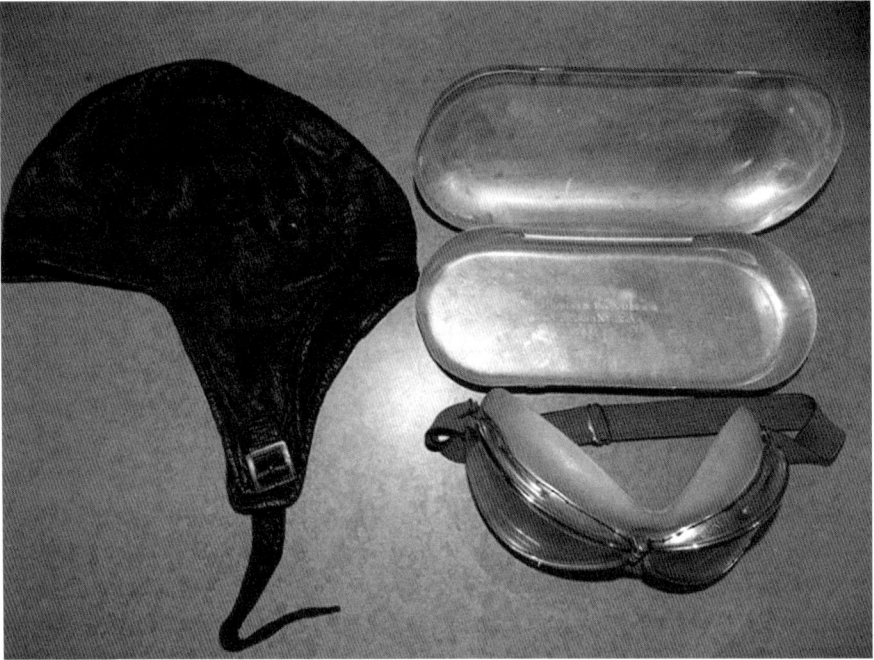

Motorcycle headgear and "rocket" goggles. *Courtesy of Michael DeBock.*

sponsor races on November 11, which was the one-year anniversary of the Great War armistice. Daly agreed, but on that morning, part of the track was underwater. The races were rescheduled, and drivers agreed to race—despite weather conditions—on the following weekend.

Weather was not the problem with the rescheduled races. First, the rescheduled race day lacked advertising, and it was late in the season. Second, the date was hastily made, so race officials were not present. Lastly, the competitors incurred multiple mechanical faults. Only Carmack's Marmon Special ran smoothly. Carmack and his mechanic Ernie Travis won all four races with ease. In the backstretch, he even slowed down to allow his competitors to catch up, only to leave them in the dust for the finish line. Carmack, who sponsored the races, was crowned the new state champion. Fred Eddy, the previous state title holder, came in second.

Despite ending the year with a lackluster race meet, the first post–Great War year was good for Rockford Driving Park. Charles Daly breathed new life into the park when no person nor other organization could, as he had overseen every imaginable transportation attraction and a hugely successful agricultural fair.

11

THE 1920 DALY ROUNDUP

*T*he first 1920s newspaper article about Rockford Driving Park concerned the Rock River Fair Association's potential purchase plans for land near West State Street. Frank M. Smith planned to subdivide his 134 acres into 660 lots. The association's members believed the subdivision plans were a good plan for them, too. If the future fairs flopped, the association could recoup losses by selling the lots. By late April, the information was found to simply be a rumor, and the Rock River Fair Association ceased operations despite huge profits and community interest. The driving park once again failed to host a continuous group or event. New direction was needed for the park.

Fred Spaulding, Winnebago County's youngest Great War veteran, pressed Rockford officials to create a municipal aviation field at driving park. Spaulding flew over France and represented Rockford at the International Aviation Congress in Chicago. He presented national maps to the Rockford Chamber of Commerce and stressed building an aerodrome, because aviation had a bright future. Airplanes provided smoother and faster rides than automobiles. Other cities like Rockford across the nation had built aerodromes. The driving park was a perfect location, because the landing field needed to be at least sixty acres (the driving park was eighty acres), flat, clear of shrubs and tree stumps, away from homes and near roads, railroads, and trolley services. There was room to build hangars and to have repair services. Spaulding also pointed out the economic boost that it would provide to the entire city, as aviators would stay at the hotels, eat at the restaurants and buy supplies. Since Rockford was near Chicago, Rockford could act as a stop on a bigger "airplane expressway." Spaulding's vision even included women, since they could quickly fly to Chicago from Rockford to shop and return for lunch. At this time, Rockford Driving Park was listed solely as an emergency landing site for aviators. The driving park was still privately owned, so the Rockford City Council took no action.

In the meantime, an auction newspaper advertisement appeared. In late April 1920, thirty-three box stalls, wire fence, wooden posts, garages, a dance floor and even the hub rail (the low wooden rail inside of the infield fence) from the driving park track were to be sold without reserve. The park was to be cleared of practically everything. The Rock River Fair Association may have wanted to raise cash to purchase the rumored new land for future fairs, or perhaps Daly needed to raise cash or simply wanted to make room for his new plans for the park. He busied himself organizing two new events. He first planned a combination of horse and automobile racing and an automobile polo match during Decoration Day weekend. The Rockford Derby was a new jockeyed race with a large purse. Fred Horey, the former automobile dirt-track champion, was first to sign up for these races. Daly contacted Sig Haugdahl to defend his title against Horey. The only problem was timing. Decoration Day weekend was the same weekend as the Indianapolis Speedway race, yet Haugdahl eventually agreed to appear. Large race purses and nationally recognized automobile drivers meant large crowds and profits.

The second event Daly announced was a Fourth of July national roundup show that featured champion cowboys and cowgirls roping and riding seventy-five horses and sixty-five steers. Slim Allen, the national "bulldogger and rope thrower," along with his wife, "Prairie Lilly" Allen, the woman champion "broncho [sic] buster," were the event headliners. Other national characters would also perform, including Princess Mohawk, who rode three horses abreast, and James Lynch, who leapt from a motorcycle or automobile to wrestle a steer to the ground. Pony Express races, relay races, bareback races, bull-riding, Roman riding and a trick rope competition were advertised. In addition to the "Wild West show" harness races, a car show and fireworks were also planned.

Daly guaranteed that spectators were taken care of, too. He increased grandstand seating to forty thousand. He hired a mechanic for spectator automobiles in need of service in case owners had driven far to the park. Parking lot attendants patrolled parking areas during the entertainment. According to the *Republic*, Daly secured a contract with the Fay Motor Bus

Company to provide thirty buses to the park. However, Daly was not the only one to think of everything and everyone.

Just as the WCTU had watched the unfolding events happening at the park in the 1890s, the Winnebago County Humane Society noted the roundup. The society believed spurs, throwing cattle on the ground by the neck and "bulldogging steers" were inhumane treatments. Frank Colehour, president of the local society, believed state and national societies would support the prevention of the "cruel" events. Colehour quickly proposed a meeting with Daly.

Daly was in Indiana contracting a new fireworks show. When he returned to Rockford on May 17, he announced that 10 percent of the roundup rodeo gate fees would be given to local charities, but not for the Winnebago County Humane Society. On May 18, Daly met Colehour and promised that none of the roundup acts was inhumane. Daly claimed long spurs were "frowned upon" by the entrants and that he signed a contract with livestock owners to return the livestock in healthy condition. In an effort to be transparent, Daly invited Colehour to be his honored guest during the event. Colehour's reply was not reported.

Automobile drivers for the Decoration Day races began arriving. Horey had raced in Rockford the previous August. Floyd Willard appeared in his Monroe (one of only four ever made). Boston's Ray LaPlante shipped his Briscoe automobile by train and was ready to test-drive it. Sig Haugdahl anticipated another Horey rematch, and the last entry was Jimmy Chy, a Chinese driver who drove a Kan San automobile. Daly had eight nationally recognized automobile racers lined up. Tickets cost fifty cents plus the war tax to pay for the talent and make a profit.

Seven races, with a total of $5,000 in purse money, were slated, along with automobile polo games. On opening day, an estimated five or six thousand attended to witness Haugdahl retain his title. On the second day, there were three harness races. Veteran drivers Fay Carney and the elderly Matt Trask returned to the track. One automobile race was run after the horse races, and local Charles Spataford won. Daly ended each day with gimmicks.

Freeport's C.W. Nelson performed as a daredevil airplane wing-walker act. He was supposed to conclude his show with a parachute jump in front of the grandstand. Instead, he missed his target and landed a half-mile northwest of it. Another gimmick was a race between an airplane, a motorcycle and an automobile. Fred Eddy drove his Oakland automobile and Claude Smith rode his motorcycle against the airplane *Betty* flown by Lieutenant Herbert E. Wilson. Neighbors around Rockford Driving Park

Claude Smith poses on a motorcycle in front of his bicycle and motorcycle shop on North Madison Street. *Courtesy of Michael DeBock.*

paused to see the plane fly and heard roaring engines whirling around the track. No report was made about which machine won. Daly's hopes of attendance and profits flourished, and he turned his attentions to the upcoming roundup.

Daly kept adding entertainments to the original roundup. Daly contracted a Galesburg aviation group to provide aerial flights over Rockford that departed from the infield. Camp Grant officials would host a military show on July 6. Units of cavalry, tanks, infantry and other military machinery and personnel were to perform maneuvers in the driving park infield. Camp Grant polo teams would play at the end of the mock battle. Daly kept contracting more and more shows to keep ahead of the competition and to make more money. Harlem Park offered fireworks and entertainers of their own over the Fourth of July weekend. Daly wanted people on the street railways to ride toward his park and not toward the competition.

Daly's Fourth of July fireworks arrived by rail on June 25, and they were loaded onto a truck. A cigarette left on one of the wooden cartons fell between the wooden slats. Suddenly, explosions were heard, and the truck driver and passenger swiftly exited the vehicle. They dumped the lit cartons onto the ground and reversed the truck. If all of the fireworks had ignited, the truck would have exploded, and the people of South Rockford would have been treated to a huge free show.

In the days leading up to the event, "fifty western characters" came to Rockford. Workers constructed animal pens, enlarged seating to accommodate forty thousand people and dug trenches for soldiers participating in reenactments. The Moss Brothers Carnival was also set up. It included ten different children's rides that posed direct competition to Harlem Park. Daly wanted everyone in Rockford and the surrounding communities to know about the activities. He ran a full-page advertisement in the *Daily Register Gazette* on June 26.

Hundreds lined the streets and were amazed as a parade of roundup performers and Camp Grant tanks traveled through the downtown business

AUTO RACES—Auto Polo
Rockford Driving Park—Sat., May 29th—Sunday, May 30th
RACES START AT 2:30.
North Main Street Cars — Fay Bus Line.   Excellent Parking Place, Men in Charge.

FAMOUS DRIVERS ENTERED	RECORD HOLDING CARS
SIG. HAUGDAHL—Track Champion.	ESSEX FIAT MONROE
FRED HOREY—Holder World's 10, 20, 25 Mile Records.	DARRAGO
FLOYD WILLARD—Light Car Champion.	BRISCO CASE
CHRIS LaPLANT, MALEY, and Other Dirt Track Stars.	and Others.

AUTO POLO

Most Exciting Game.

Full Game Each Day.

Pacific Coast Champions

vs.

All Americans

Special Memorial Day — Monday, May 31st
Airplane Flights — Parachute Jumps — Horse Racing — Harness and Running Races Start at 3 P. M.

Advertisement from *Morning Star,* June 27, 1920.

district on July 3. During the day, the performers practiced. One rider, who had joined his company just the previous day, was injured when the horse he rode reared and fell backward on him. He was taken to the Camp Grant field hospital located on the park grounds, where he remained unconscious for a while. At dusk, 150 horses and cattle were unloaded by train and stampeded into the infield. A Camp Grant searchlight spotlighted the scene. Tickets for the roundup were sold at downtown businesses on both sides of the river. Huge crowds were expected, and they came.

People went to Harlem Park. They had picnics in Fairgrounds and Blackhawk Parks. However, during the three days of the roundup, eight thousand people visited the driving park. Infantry charged behind Whippet tanks and cowboys threw themselves off their horses and tackled steers to the ground at blinding speed. The carnival entertained children, and the *Morning Star* journalist was pleased that the music for the merry-go-round had been changed to a different tune. Attendees witnessed it all on opening day.

The patriotism of July 4 did not end. July 5 was considered "Camp Grant Day" at the roundup. At the beginning of the day, Brigadier General George Bell Jr. awarded the Distinguished Service Cross to George S. Johnson (company K, Sixteenth Infantry) from Rockford in front of his hometown crowd. Johnson fought in Germany during the Great War and "bagged four Germans" while fighting in Fleuville, France, on October 4, 1918. His unit was prevented from advancing due to a German machine gun. Johnson crawled toward the enemy gun crew and, with his sergeant, was able to capture four German machine gun crew prisoners. It was the first time a soldier had been decorated in Rockford since June 1918. After the ceremony concluded, soldiers reenacted a Great War battle for the attendees. A Camp Grant polo team contest was planned to end the day.

When the fireworks, troops and cowboys had all vanished from the park, Daly found himself in court. Colehour, the local humane society president, had him and the manager of the roundup charged with animal cruelty due to the cowboys/girls use of spurs and for "bulldogging" events. Daly and the manager paid a ten-dollar fine, which could have been worse, but the judge who heard the case had attended the event and enjoyed it. On July 7, the next day, Daly again appeared in court. The manager of concessions, Mr. Davis, was angry that Daly had not paid him. Daly supposedly told Davis that he would pay him to provide meals for the Camp Grant band that played throughout the Fourth of July weekend. Daly either forgot to pay Davis or thought that Davis would forget. Daly hired T.E. Gill to represent him in court. Daly testified that he would have paid Davis if he simply asked him to and that it was not necessary for him to be dragged into court. Daly paid Davis twelve dollars and fifty cents, and the debt was officially settled. The court date was not the worst that Daly faced in the aftermath of the roundup.

On July 11, Andrew Rotello practiced racing his automobile at the driving park. He and his mechanic, Charles Bentley, had just completed their third lap in fifty-eight seconds. Daly did not approve of Rotello practicing on the track and repeatedly yelled, "Get off the track!" When they came around the first turn, Daly tried to set a trap. Daly stood firm in the middle of the track and held a line of barbed wire wrapped around a stump. Daly must have wanted to puncture Rotello's tires. Rotello's vehicle was going so fast that there was no time to avoid Daly. The left front tire struck Daly, and he was thrown to the side of the track. Rotello and Bentley were thrown from the automobile as it flipped over, and they sustained no injuries. Daly suffered an extremely bruised head, broken right arm, fractured right hand, dislocated thumb, broken leg, twisted ankle and from potential internal injuries. Deputy Sheriff Henry Cassidy was at the track at the time but did not witness the crash. Rotello claimed that he had Daly's permission to practice there. Cassidy took the barbed wire for evidence, and no charges were filed. Daly made no comment while recuperating and continued to sign future event contracts.

The roundup aftermath drama continued. Teenager William Clow worked for a New Milford farmer. After he attended the roundup, Clow developed a plan. He returned to the farm where he worked, stole resources and left with the cowboys. The farmer reported the theft to the police. Sheriff Baldwin tracked the group to Ohio, where Clow was found among them and forced to return to New Milford. He was placed on probation and returned the stolen items to his employer. Once he had made enough money, he could return to the cowboy group if he wished.

Everette and Dorothy Gigous were two children who attended the "sham battle" at the driving park. Everette pocketed some "dummy shells" (which contain gunpowder) to take home to North Court Street. Then, he threw the shells into a lit stove. He and his sister were cut by flying metal fragments and were given quick medical attention. Their wounds eventually healed.

Finally, by late July, attention was brought back to the track's original racing purpose. The Rockford Motorcycle Racing Association signed a contract with Daly to host a motorcycle meet featuring nationally known riders. The program of events listed five-, ten- and twenty-five-mile professional races, with the professional-national two-mile race to be held at the end of the event on Sunday. A bicycle race and a sidecar race were held for locals to participate in. Gene Walker (Indian) and Jim Davis (Harley-Davidson) were extreme rivals who each had no idea that the other had signed up to ride until they met in downtown Rockford. People took notice of their arrival and rushed to the track to see them practice. Even the baseball column from the *Daily Register Gazette* ran a special poem by "Leo Lens" about Walker taking turns at the track on July 23, 1920:

> *To Mister Razz Berry:*
> *Dear Sir:-*
> *When it comes to our getting killed taking good fortygrafts of careless youths racing on motorcycles at the driving park we lose all interest in photo graphy. Gene Walker burned the whiskers off our graflex when he skidded around that turn at 50 mph. Besides that, he scared one long geared photographer out of six years' growth. So if you want any more fortygraphs, yelp for the sub picture-shooter. He's married and consequently doesn't care what happens to him.*

Prize money worth $2,000 was on the line. Four other riders would take their positions on the starting line. Tickets for the two-day racing event cost seventy-five cents plus the war tax. Spectators could park their automobiles in the infield for free and watch the five-, ten- and twenty-five-mile races while seated in them. In between races, a locals-only bicycle race and sidecar race were planned. The sidecar races were held, but the bicycle races were cancelled due to a lack of entries. Prizes were offered instead of monetary rewards. The winner of the two-mile race on Sunday, the second day of racing, would hold the 1920 national championship title. In the morning, all of the riders made practice laps and fine-tuned their engines. Davis fell off his motorcycle during a practice run while going forty-five miles per hour in the first curve. He was lucky and only had bruises and cuts. He raced later in the day.

Walker won all three races. Davis and Walker tied for the fastest lap at 51.1 seconds. Walker had stiff competition, though. Ludlow, the other Harley-Davidson rider, tried to take the outside on Walker in the five-mile race. While in a turn, he slid into a broadside but did not lose balance or control of his vehicle. A burst of dust kicked up, and Ludlow was only a hair behind Walker, in second place, when they crossed the finish line. The local sidecar race was exciting, too. Camp Grant's Hamel was in the lead of the ten-mile race when he sputtered out along the backstretch in the third lap. The race was now between Sheriff Warren and Heine from Freeport. The lead shifted between the two until the last lap. In the homestretch curve, Warren passed Heine and won. At the end of the day, 1,500 spectators had been thrilled, and excitement grew overnight, because the next day was the race for the national championship. Harley-Davidson shipped new motorcycles to Davis and Ludlow for them to ride that evening.

Walker left all of the other competitors in the dust on the second day and again won all the events. Davis was passed by Ludlow, who led a race shortly until Walker let his engine roar at full throttle to the cheering crowds. Walker set the 1920 two-mile race national championship time in 1:40. A huge crowd of eight thousand people lined the entire track for the second day of races. In the first lap of the five-mile race, Waldorf Corn (Walker's Indian teammate rider) lost control of his motorcycle trying to help Walker maintain his lead while traveling at fifty miles per hour. He was thrown through the barbed-wire fence and hit an automobile. His arm was cut up, and he was bruised but otherwise in good shape. He withdrew from the rest of the day's races. Local Rockford drivers who left the park must have been inspired by the driving park races, as there were many accidents reported in the city that weekend.

Rockfordians could not get enough fast-speed racing. Two weeks after the motorcycle races, one-day amateur automobile races—once again sponsored by the Rockford Motor Racing Association—were scheduled for the park. It was better to race and speed at the park instead of on the streets of Rockford. Automobile racers from Rockford, Beloit, St. Charles and Woodstock entered. Rivalries built between the local men as they sped around the track. Dust floated everywhere, but track officials assured everyone that the track would be sprinkled before the races. However, being covered in dust was only a part of the racing excitement, and it was expected as a "badge of honor" when a spectator returned home.

Meanwhile, amid the planning for the automobile racing, a new airplane taxi service was in the process of being installed in the park. The representative of the service, Budd Gage, proposed that an airplane should race an automobile during the amateur meet to develop interest. The company also employed aerial stuntmen who hung from Curtiss Airplane wings and gave airplane rides to thrill-seekers. Rockford was a central location for many midwestern cities, and the service seemed to be a very profitable idea. It was so profitable that Gage developed headquarters at the Nelson Hotel and had two planes immediately sent to Rockford with top pilots. Fred Spaudling, who clamored for the service at the beginning of 1920, must have been pleased, or perhaps he had written the Du Jardin Aero Company a letter, and it was not mentioned in the newspapers.

The Rockford area was in the middle of a drought. The sprinkling wagon made its own laps around the track on the morning of August 8, 1920. The local drivers took in many practice laps, as local bragging rights and track records were on the line. The crowd began to assemble in the grandstand. The drivers and their mechanics fine-tuned their engines. At 2:30 p.m., the starter called for the first event, the five-mile free-for-all. The engines roared, and the crowd began to feel their hearts pump with anticipation. The flag was dropped, and the automobiles lurched forward from the starting line. The thrill of racing did not last long for H. Kolhert. Early in the race, he blew a tire, which wrenched the wheel completely off of his vehicle in the southeast corner of the track. The race was stopped. Doctors Howard and Burdick got into Burdick's Buick and raced toward Kolhert's vehicle to check on him. Both Kolhert and his mechanic, Joe Nelson, were unharmed. Kolhert's vehicle was quickly repaired, and the race was restarted. Not long after the restart, Walter Hahn (a St. Charles driver) missed the northwest curve. He and his mechanic ripped through the barbed wire and plowed through a lot of dirt off of the track. Hahn suffered cuts on his back, and the mechanic suffered a burn on his hip. Kolhert could not make the turn, either, and his vehicle ripped toward Hahn's. The doctors sped to the scene of the crash, but Dr. Burdick must not have moved his automobile far enough off of the track. The dust was thick as smoke. Charlie Spatafora avoided the doctor's automobile but made a lot of dust behind him. Ed Johnson and his brother Joseph (his mechanic) trailed Spatafora, breathing in his dust. When the Johnson brothers came around the corner of the track, they could not see the doctor's automobile, which was parked with its rear end slightly on the track. With the Johnson brothers traveling at sixty-five miles per hour, Dr. Burdick sensed what was about to happen. He quickly motioned to the small crowd that had assembled around the crash site and his automobile to run to safety. The Johnson vehicle struck the rear end of the doctor's automobile like a thunderclap. Both Johnson brothers were thrown into the air. Ed fell on the track, and Joseph was thrown far away. Race officials frantically tried to flag the other drivers to stop, but the dust clouds prevented them from being seen. In total, four cars were disabled in various places near the track. It was the largest automobile wreck the spectators at driving park had ever witnessed.

When the smoke cleared, the doctor's Buick was a complete loss. Ed Johnson had his right shoulder dislocated and right arm fractured in three places. Kolhert had a severely bruised chest from whamming into his steering column. The rest of the drivers and mechanics involved suffered cuts and bruises. The rest of the day's races followed once the debris was cleared. Spatafora won all of the races in a clean sweep. No drivers gave any comments or raised any issues. They all knew that the doctor's automobile would come out onto the track once an accident occurred, and they all knew that that corner of the racetrack was not banked and was the most dangerous corner of the track. They also agreed that something had to be done in the name of safety to keep spectators from crowding around the corners. The excitement and thrill of racing had been replaced with fear and trepidation. The park returned to hosting a safer event.

On August 23, beginning around 8:00 a.m., people began to line the streets of downtown Rockford to see the big Ringling Bros. Circus parade. They patiently continued to wait. The noon whistle blew in the distance. Children grew impatient. Soon, word came that the parade would not occur. A parade was planned to march through the streets of Rockford but was cancelled because the circus had performed in Chicago and arrived in Rockford too late. The circus officials had to make a decision: either go through with the parade or cancel a performance. They were not about to lose money, so they chose to cancel the parade. Once they arrived in the railyard, they quickly began the long trek toward the park. The circus did not simply unload off of the dock alongside the park, because there were too many railcars. Finally, tents were propped up in the driving park infield. Exotic animals and 1,200 entertainers and crew members were there. Multiple shows were staged, and a cross-section of Rockford's entire population attended. Yet again, the park had reinvented itself for other purposes in order to stay viable.

The Rockford Motor Racing Association decided to hold another one-day racing event at Driving Park on September 26. This time, the majority of the racing officials were replaced with "competent" officials to prevent another rash of accidents and injuries. Many of the same drivers signed up for the events, and officials vowed to "patrol the track" with Camp Grant guards to prevent spectators from crowding around the curves. Heats were run the day before race day to eliminate competitors whose automobiles could not complete a lap around the track at sixty-five miles per hour. The track had been oiled and scraped. Drivers had practiced at high speeds for a week, but when race time rolled around at 1:30 p.m., the skies poured

AUTOMOBILE RACES!

Rockford Driving Park, Today, Sept. 26th

Races Start at 2 P.M.--Veteran Drivers--Four Events

$300 In Cash Prizes Offered — One to 25 Miles for Cups and Money Awards

SPEED! SPEED!

17 Entries From Rockford and Surrounding Territory

Twenty Mounted Guards From Camp Grant to Preserve Order

A clean-cut gathering of well-known veteran drivers who always aim to "clip time from all previous records." Come; See; Be satisfied of the sincerity and ability of Rockford's local racing organization to give the highest class, exciting sport in Auto Races.

Rockford Motor Racing Association

Rockford Motor Racing Association advertising picture. *From* Morning Star, *July 31, 1921.*

rain on the starting line. Spectators and drivers alike would have to wait another week.

The next day, the clouds must have broken long enough to allow Robert Blair to take Ciseretta Smothers into the air in his 260-horsepower airplane. She then wrote a testimonial of her experience. Apparently, she had practiced for the flight by taking an elevator from the top floor of a building to the basement. During the flight, she experienced no ill effects and encouraged others in Rockford to see their city from the air.

Finally, race day came on October 2, 1920. Conditions were fair. About 2,500 spectators came from Rockford and the surrounding area. Safety and speed were the buzzwords of the day. Gretchen Zick and a friend of hers came from Clinton, Wisconsin, to watch the races. They parked their Ford around one of the south turns, sixty feet away from the track, and sat on the radiator of the automobile. The first event was against time. Joe Hanson, in a Ford Special, turned a lap in fifty-seven seconds flat. Andrew Rotello won the five- and ten-mile races. The last race event was the twenty-five-mile race. In the seventeenth lap, Rotello's luck ran out. His right rear wheel tore off of his automobile in the south turn of the track and spun over the track fence. Zick probably had no time to react. The wheel hit her Ford and knocked her off of the radiator or it hit her on the hip (the reports conflicted). Rotello had been in the lead. He maintained control of his automobile, and the other racers were flagged to a stop. Dr. Howard tended to Zick at the Rockford Hospital and treated her fractured right leg and sprained ankle. Due to Zick's experience, track safety concerns were reviewed once again.

By the fall of 1920, Charles Lee Daly must have recuperated enough from being hit by Rotello's automobile in July to leave the park and the Rockford area. He had ushered in a flurry of activity like the park had not seen since it opened in 1890. Rockford Driving Park had become a center for all modes of transportation and for community events never seen before, such as the Great War reenactment. The park was stifled without him, because no major events other than the October Northern Illinois Livestock Breeders Association pure-breed hog sale were planned for the rest of the year.

The park was quiet for the winter.

At the end of January 1921, Frank Lee took his horse Flash out for a test drive. The horse trotted well, and Lee decided to train his horse at the park. One horse. That was it. Traditionally, Decoration Day had been a time for racing in the park. In 1921, there was nothing. The park needed someone with the ability and motivation to organize events. Charles Daly had provided the park with direction and profitable organization. The park's future was again in jeopardy. Individuals or organizations would have to arrange their own separate contracts with Julius Graham to lease the park for either racing or entertainment.

Al. G. Barnes Circus was the first organization to lease the park from Graham in July 1921. The circus train had fifty-two cars and boasted of possessing the nation's largest elephant, Tusko (supposedly outsizing Ringling's Jumbo). The circus gave two performances and also arranged a parade through Rockford. Barnes's circus was unique, because all performances were animal acts, which meant no acrobats, fire-eaters and the like. Barnes's circus made a profit and planned to return to Rockford the next year.

The Rockford Motor Racing Association announced that racing would return after the circus left town. The association had arranged a lease for an undetermined length of time at the driving park for themselves. A new wooden fence was built around the track to ensure spectator safety, and entries were being filed. Andrew Rotello was impatient for race day. To better the fifty-seven-second lap record, he drove his Ford around the track in fifty-six seconds, achieving a new track record two days before the official races began. In addition to the stopwatch, he would face other drivers from Stockton, Elgin, Beloit and St. Charles on race day.

At Kishwaukee Park, the Camp Grant Fifty-Third Infantry baseball team played the Rockford Orioles. The Orioles beat the infantry team 10–1. The game lacked attendance, because spectators were at Rockford Driving Park watching races instead. As many as five hundred spectator parking places were available in a field west of the park. A sprinkler truck, meant to prevent dust from flying into the faces of drivers and spectators, failed to appear. About 2,500 spectators came to enjoy the races. Rotello could not beat his fifty-six-second lap. In fact, he seemed incapable of finding a functional automobile on race day. His first automobile threw two tires, his second stripped a clutch gear and he broke a rocker arm in another. Joslyn threw two tires in the same race. Due to numerous mechanical and tire issues, the races were sluggish, with average lap times at well over a minute. At least the spectators, as well as the racers, went home uninjured this time. Safety for all finally seemed to have been attained.

12

AERIAL DEPARTURE

*D*uring the 1920s, many Americans belonged to social clubs. Some clubs were devoted to providing community service, organizing veterans, promoting religion, advancing education or helping newly arrived immigrants. According to Geneva (New York) Historical Society archivist Karen Osburn in a blog entry entitled "Clubs, Associations, Organizations: Networking in the 1920s": "In the days before, television, computers, and digital social networks these organizations were how you were entertained, met people with similar interests, established business connections and got to know your neighbors." Rockford—like Geneva, New York, during the 1920s—also had numerous active social clubs.

The Knights Templar had a conclave in Rockford. According to the current Knights Templar website, the organization is "a Christian-oriented fraternal organization and an integral part of the Masonic Fraternity." Arthur A. Johnson, head of the Knights Templar conclave motor transport committee in 1921, pleaded with Rockford automobile owners to aid the organization from August 15–20 with at least five hundred vehicles. The annual Illinois Grand Commandery Conclave of the Knights was to be held in Rockford. Local hotels reserved one thousand rooms, as ten thousand knights were expected to arrive. Rockford automobile drivers were generally favorable to Johnson, but Johnson still worried. Automobiles were needed for a parade and for a special sightseeing tour of the area's points of interest for Lady Knights. While in Rockford, the Knights leased the driving park and contracted the Tri-City Aerial Transportation Company to perform racing shows and stunts on August 16 and 17 for its visiting members. They featured races between automobiles, airplanes, bicycles and horses. Children were encouraged to sign up for the two-mile bike race. In addition to the races, they had performers who would entertain and thrill crowds.

Vilbert "Bud" Bridgens was a performer who jumped from a speeding automobile or motorcycle and could catch a rope ladder hanging from an airplane flying overhead. Bridgens also performed a trapeze act on top of airplane wings in flight and could jump from one plane to another. Jack Towers could ascend three thousand feet into the air by clenching his teeth on a rope attached to a hot-air balloon or parachute-jump four thousand feet from a balloon and safely land (he had done so previously at Harlem Park). R.H. Bloxham and G.R. Van Dyke were former Royal and U.S. Air Force pilots who could push their machines to their limits.

W.B. Rothwell gave an interview with the *Daily Register Gazette* in which he informed the reporter that new attractions had been added to the "Flying Circus" since his friend, Omar Locklear, had perished in an accident. Rothwell stated with a laugh, "We use no straps in our trapeze work, and no parachutes. If we slip—well, it will only happen once." He added, "We fly close to the ground so the people can see that we do not use straps or other safety devices." The *Morning Star* reported that days earlier in Iowa, stunts like the ones to be performed in Rockford resulted in the deaths of two performers. The reporter added a subtitle to his article: "Not mere fun festival." Again, safety was an issue at Rockford Driving Park.

The Knights arrived in droves, and Rockford was ill-prepared. Johnson continued to worry, because only two hundred automobile owners volunteered to provide transportation. He needed another three hundred. There were not enough rooms in the hotels, and as a result, people were sent to Camp Grant. Wives were separated from their husbands in the barracks. The women found the barracks very masculine, so they decorated them. When dinner was served, the men received their meals first, while the women waited. Some women grew tired of waiting and joined the men. Fay Bus Company buses constantly ran between downtown Rockford and Camp Grant. While passing by the Murphy & Fitzgerald Funeral Parlor, the Knights saw a dubious sign in the window that read, "Welcome, Sir Knights." Rockford's restaurants, hotels and streets were filled with visitors who added to the Rockford economy.

After rain postponed the aerial show from August 16 to August 17, people enjoyed a promotional parade and brass band traveling through the Rockford streets. Meanwhile, Bridgens prepared for his big aerial jump.

The day before, he had commented to a reporter about his parachute. "That old sack is cookoo; it's going to open one of these days and then its curtains for me." Bridgens worked on aerial stunts for two months and rapidly wished to return to the movie business, because daredevil work was monotonous. At 2:15 p.m., Bridgens climbed aboard Al Bloxham's plane, piloted by R.A. Van Hake along with Mrs. Bridgens. The plane climbed to between 1,400 and 2,000 feet in altitude, and Van Hake gave Bridgens the signal. Bridgens planned to jump a little ahead of the driving park, because he wanted to land in the park. "Bet you won't see me land," he shouted to his wife. "Bet I will," she shouted back. He jumped off the plane. W.H. Sauber's family stood on their porch to see the stunt, along with several other families along Rockton Avenue and Glenwood. To everyone's horror, Bridgens's prophecy about his parachute came true. It did not open properly. Onlookers watched him plummet from the sky. Van Hake stated, "I immediately saw it did not open and believed that Bud fought the chute all the way down in an effort to open it." He landed in a cornfield belonging to John H. Prial (a police officer) in the Glenwood Subdivision west of the park. A passing car stopped, and residents who watched him fall picked him up, but he was lifeless. Van Hake landed the plane as quickly as he could. Mrs. Bridgens was hysterical and was taken to the hospital only to see her husband dead from a crushed chest. The body compressed the ground for several inches.

At the inquiry, many things were revealed. Bridgens's parachute was inspected and found to be incorrectly packed. The rope used for the parachute was not strong enough to release the chute out of the sack in which it was contained. Bloxham quickly stated that he did not give Van Hake or Bridgens permission to attempt the stunt. Van Hake stated that Bridgens simply wanted to practice the stunt to ensure that it could be done correctly before the crowds.

Bridgens had served at Camp Grant as a guard in 1917, with Company H, 131st Infantry, Thirty-Third Division, and was survived by his wife and several Rock Island area relatives. The cause of Bridgens's death was officially a crushed chest and broken neck, as declared by coroner Fred C. Olson. He was twenty-five years old and had only been married for a month and a half. When news of Bridgens's death reached Chicago, Audrey Bridgens traveled to Rockford to see her husband. In August 1919, Bud Bridgens left her seven months pregnant, and he had not seen Audrey since. While staying at the Nelson Hotel, Audrey and Bridgens's mother, Mrs. Gage, met the second "Mrs. Bridgens." The second Mrs. Bridgens knew that Bridgens was previously married but believed he was completely divorced from Audrey. This was not the case. His mother was stunned, too, because she was not informed by her son that he had remarried. Both wives exchanged sympathies and relinquished all rights to their husband to his mother. Bridgens was buried in Oak Ridge Cemetery in Sandwich, Illinois, with all military rights.

The show must go on, because two thousand spectators filled the grandstand on August 20 to see aerial stunts and local drivers racing. The two stunts that Bridgens was supposed to complete were scratched, and Wade B. Rothwell replaced him. It took six attempts for Rothwell, standing on a racing automobile, to grab the ladder dangling from the airplane, but he successfully completed the stunt. The crowd left the park grounds satisfied. Rothwell's luck ran out the next day. While attempting to grab the ladder while standing on the back of Sam Mattioli's speeding roadster, Rothwell lost his grip on the ladder and fell off the back of the automobile. Rothwell's body slammed into the track. Van Hake, who was again the pilot, immediately landed the plane and came to Rothwell's aid as soon as he could. When doctors tended to him, Rothwell was unconscious but not seriously injured. Half an hour later, he was lying in bed at the Nelson Hotel and told reporters what went wrong while smoking a cigarette. A strong crosswind prevented Van Hake from perfectly aligning the plane with the automobile. The ladder moved unexpectedly as Rothwell jumped to grab it. Meanwhile, rumors floated around that he had died, because everyone was remembering what happened to Bridgens.

During the same show, Jack Towers parachuted from a hot-air balloon and accidentally landed in the same cornfield where Bridgens died. He had not accounted for the swift winds and descended quicker than he anticipated. He sustained minor injuries after his stunt. After the Rockford stunt show, Rothwell and Van Hake both quit Bloxham's employ (and daredevil work) forever. Rothwell thought he was lucky, and Van Hake believed it was simply a "nerve-racking week." Bloxham returned to the Rock Falls area to regroup his entire company. The races that were held that Sunday were probably less remembered. Claude Smith, on his Indian, handily won the motorcycle race, and Andrew Rotello won both of the automobile races.

The track would not remain empty for many days after the tragic aerial events. Many Rockford drivers and riders had won prizes in races in Woodstock and in Elgin and wanted more. An Elgin driver named Sensor had beaten several Rockford drivers, and revenge was in order. Sensor agreed to come to Rockford. Races were to be held at Rockford Driving

Claude Smith (*left*) and Harland Krause (*right*). This picture may have been taken in the homestretch of the park. *Courtesy of Michael DeBock.*

Park on Labor Day. There were picnics, baseball games, a tennis match and Pecatonica horse racing at the newly established Winnebago Agricultural Society Fair, and Sammy Mandel fought in Aurora that same weekend. To entice spectators, the driving park admission price was lowered from the one-dollar general charge to seventy-five cents.

Despite many other entertainments offered on the same day, a throng of two thousand spectators arrived. According to the *Republic*, only half of the crowd paid admission. H.E. McCann, A.W. Seipp, ? Fairhead and Everett Gigous were a few of the spectators who lined the fence to watch the races. They came to see the action but had no idea that they would be part of it. During the twenty-mile free-for-all race, in the fifth lap, Sarver's automobile threw a rear wheel. Seipp anticipated that the wheel was headed toward him and tried to protect himself. Nevertheless, the wheel struck him hard "in the thigh and groin." Two minutes later, Joe Johnson's automobile skidded in the homestretch and lost a right wheel. It flew toward the same fence, this time striking McCann. Originally, McCann's leg was believed to be fractured, but it was later discovered that it was only severely cut and bruised. Fairhead and Gigous were knocked down. Their clothing was torn, and they were bruised, but they were not taken to the hospital. Park security had, again, not taken safety precautions, but they stated that they felt no responsibility toward the injured because they had not paid admission.

Besides the "flying wheel" injuries in the homestretch, the races were exciting. Howard "Runt" Ryan (on a Harley-Davidson) set an amateur record for the ten-mile motorcycle race, averaging sixty-seven miles per hour. He was followed by Conroy (on an Indian) and Smith, who blew a cylinder in the last lap. Andrew Rotello defeated the Elgin driver in the ten-mile Ford Special race and also won the twenty-mile race, followed by Sarver in second, Johnson in third and Hahn from St. Charles in fourth.

After the crowds left the park, it remained empty for the winter. Meanwhile, the Pecatonica Driving Park Association held harness and jockeyed races in the fall. As 1922 began, the Young Business Man's Association and the Farm Bureau stirred discussion about another agricultural fair to be held in Rockford. George Rubin offered sixty-five acres next to the Central Park Gardens if he could be granted the concession rights. Rockford Driving Park was proposed as the venue because the previous and overwhelmingly successful fair had been held there in 1919. By May, twenty-five prestigious county citizens met at the Elks Club to discuss the matter. It was agreed that both Pecatonica and Rockford could hold agricultural fairs and not be "enemies." Henry Needham stated that the fair association could rent the park for $3,000 annually and have an $80,000 option to purchase the park. A five-day fair would be held and bring 100,000 paid admissions for a projected profit of between $15,000 and $20,000 after initial starting investments of $40,000. Another meeting was scheduled. However, this once again proved to be just talk. Decoration Day came and went with no races held at the park.

Andy Rotello with his mechanic Ralph Joslyn; Howard "Runt" Ryan on his Harley-Davidson. *From* Daily Register-Gazette, *September 6, 1921.*

The Rockford Automobile Racing Association had attempted to lease the park for races in August, but a deal could not be struck. Frank Johnson, manager of Central Park Gardens, proposed building a new racetrack north of Kent Creek. The length of the track was not specified, but the idea appealed to the association. Again, the future of the park was in jeopardy, and nothing could be agreed upon.

13.

WHAT'S NEXT?

*I*n October 1922, Jesse O. Marshall, originally from Denver, opened the Rockford Riding Academy's school (later renamed the Marshall Riding Academy) at Rockford Driving Park. He had fourteen horses, including his two show horses, which could jump high obstacles, stabled on the grounds. The track was used for training, and the horses were rented for evenings. Marshall advertised for his riding academy in the newspapers and also had racing on his mind, because he planned to bring it back to the park in 1923.

In May 1923, Julius Graham made additional money by leasing some land north of the driving park to the Rockford United Soccer Club. The soccer team previously had a limited schedule because they lacked a field. With the driving park lease, the Rockford team planned to host a Chicago team. A group of Rockford Swedish players formed their own team and also proposed to play the United team. Soccer, as a sport, began to grow rapidly after the Great War because the returning soldiers played it in Europe. The *Morning Star* believed it would eventually become as popular as football.

In June, the park was threatened just outside its gates. The Osborne Oil Company had four fifteen-thousand-gallon gasoline tanks located just east of the park gates. A switch engine had passed along the tracks, and sparks from its wheels caused a grass fire, which steadily approached the tanks. Oil company employees acted quickly as they removed their coats and grabbed brooms and buckets of water. The fire department later assisted. Fire had "licked" the tanks and scorched the paint but came no further as far as causing massive destruction. According to the *Morning Star*, one of the tanks had a small leak around the base that increased the intensity of the fire.

In July, the Ringling Bros. and Barnum & Bailey Circus were both slated to come to the park. Rockford was the only city in Illinois outside of Chicago that the circus performed in that year. However, Marshall planned horse racing before then. The racing card was ambitious, too. There would be four harness races, four riding races and one horse-jumping exhibition. Horse entries came from the surrounding area (twenty-four in all). Out of the seven riding horses entered, one was jockeyed by Jesse Marshall's daughter Kathryn Marshall. Kathryn was only fourteen years old and rode a horse named Flirt. Beloit's William Pearson was eighty-three years old and entered his horse. For years, horsemen had clamored for a half-mile track to be built. Now, it seemed that the track had been halved for half-mile races (perhaps Mitchell had done this?). The grandstand could accommodate between five hundred and two thousand fans. There was free parking for automobiles. Not unlike his predecessors, Marshall hired airplane aerialists and a band to entertain spectators between races. Newspaper journalists wondered if Rockford would support an entertainment that was once in demand.

A crowd of one thousand spectators came to the park on July 14. The admission price was reasonably set at fifty cents for adults and twenty-five cents for children. It was a Saturday, the weather held in favor of racing and the racing was worth the admission price, because all of the races were exciting. In the second heat of the first race, two horses collided in the backstretch. The drivers were only scratched. The accident allowed Beloit's Homer Amundson, who drove Robert Dillion, to drive the fastest paced mile in driving park history. Amundson made a clean sweep of all of the first event heats and won a new sulky but acted as a showman in the last heat race by pulling Robert Dillion back to create a closer race. Two Rockford horses were scratched before the second event races even began.

The second event featured driver William Pearson, a Civil War veteran who once raced with the nationally known Bud Doble. In the first heat, Pearson lost. However, Pearson won the next three heats. In the last heat race, Pearson's horse paced in third place as the field rounded the homestretch. Pearson's horse had enough to energy to win by a nose. The crowd erupted as Pearson flashed them a smile.

The last event was the riding event. Kathryn Marshall won the first heat in 1:01 but came in fourth and fifth in the other heats. Another horse, Jazz Band, owned by her father, was awarded first-place race honors because he won first in the second heat and second in the third heat. Crowds were expected to reach two thousand for the next day of racing. However, no newspaper reports exist about that day's racing. Either the weather was poor and the races were not run, or the races were canceled for unknown reasons.

These races held on July 14, 1923, were the last horse races ever held at the park. A track record, an eighty-three-year-old Civil War veteran winner and a female jockey also made them special. J.O. Marshall believed that future race events could be organized if interest existed, but that interest never came. Marshall's riding academy existed at the park until the end of 1924. Later, the sound of hoofbeats instead came from circus horses.

The Ringling Bros. and Barnum & Bailey Circus returned to the park on July 21 and held shows on July 23. The circus train stopped on the Chicago, Milwaukee and St. Paul tracks along the park at 4:00 a.m. and began to unload. The circus was like a small town on rails, because there were 1,571 performers (100 of whom were clowns), 785 horses, 28 camels and 1,009 caged animals. Children from the surrounding area were excited. Attendance at the circus was expected to peak at 25,000 (but the great tent could only hold a maximum of 16,000). The *Morning Star* published a lengthy article that gave details about the specific acts. However, the chief of police, A.E. Bargren, issued a stern warning on the front page of the *Republic*—not to children but to housewives.

> *Housewives are urged by Chief of Police A.E. Bargren to put away their valuables where thieves and crooks and other wayfarers who follow circuses won't be able to get them. Keep your homes securely locked, and ring for the police when any itinerant peddlers call at your home Monday.*
>
> *While the Barnum & Bailey and Ringling Bros. circus will not tolerate dishonesty of any kind in its organization, it is generally known that every circus has a following of crooks who are not connected with the circus in any way. The circus comes to Rockford from Chicago, and will have a greater following than usual. Rockford housewives should take extraordinary precautions.*
>
> *Housewives should keep their doors locked at all times. Fakers and peddlers will call at the houses in the residence districts. If no one is home, they will try doors and windows in an effort to enter. With the house securely locked, they will be unable to get in and the crook will not dare tarry long for fear of detection. In case a faker or peddler comes to the door while the housewife is in he should not be allowed to enter. Keep him outside.*

Instead of promoting the circus for family fun, Bargren turned the circus into a nightmare. It was no matter, though, because people came in droves. Arthur Hommena, a Rockford policeman, directed traffic at Elm and South Main Streets and was surrounded by automobiles coming into town to see the circus. He was hit by George Gustafson's rented automobile as he and his girlfriend traveled to the circus. Pedestrians took Hommena to a local store for first aid. He had no broken bones and returned to his post, stating that "the only way they [automobiles] would advance was over his dead body."

The city streets were empty as citizens attended the circus without reservation, because many businesses closed for it. The circus attracted twenty-nine thousand people (almost half of the city's population)—one of the largest crowds to ever attend a single-day event in Rockford history. Even Chief Bargren changed his tune. "There's something about a circus crowd entirely different from anything else in the world—they're good natured, slow to respond to direction from traffic officers and somewhat childish no matter what their age." Hardly any police reports were made while the circus was in town. The circus gave two performances—one in the afternoon and one in the evening. The entire Ringling Bros. and Barnum & Bailey Circus was then reloaded onto the circus trains and left, headed toward Janesville, by midnight.

In August, a completely different organization leased the park. The 1920s are considered by many historians to be the "Roaring Twenties." This era was a period of economic growth, prosperity and social change. However, many negative social trends also were strengthened at this time. The Ku Klux Klan was originally developed by Nathan Bedford Forrest after the Civil War. During Reconstruction, the period of time following the Civil War, the KKK was weakened by federal enforcement. In 1915, the motion picture *The Birth of a Nation* reignited the "Second Klan," and throughout the 1920s and 1930s, the organization gained members in the thousands. Rockford was no exception. Though the Klan is mostly known for discriminating against African Americans, Rockford's Klan members stood against Jews, Catholics and immigrants, because Rockford's African American population was minute. The KKK wanted to hold a rally at the park over September 7–8 because it was centrally located between five states and did not waste time. A Chicago construction firm was contracted to build a new temporary grandstand in the north end of the infield to accommodate twenty-five thousand unrobed spectators. In front of the grandstand, there would be seating for thousands more. The stage, a sixty-foot-tall replica of Stone Mountain and an electrified cross were built at the south end of the infield. Though the lease was signed and approved by Julius Graham, the Rockford Chamber of Commerce did not completely approve of the KKK's activities. The chamber stated that it would not lend the KKK any assistance, because they were unclear who constituted its membership or what it stood for. Others in Rockford also disapproved, because the *Morning Star* reported, "Threatened organized opposition to the Klan meeting has not developed here, but many unofficial statements unfavorable to the convention have been made by influential persons." The rally organizers believed that the event would bring between thirty and fifty thousand people to Rockford.

The Klan's official statement was: "In a showing of strength that will stagger the nation, the first midwest klankraft konklave will be held in Rockford on September 7 & 8 at Driving Park." The Imperial Wizard, Dr. H.W. Evans, phoned long distance to inform local authorities that he and his staff would attend the Rockford pageant along with other high-ranking Klan authorities from across the United States. Special trains and automobile groups were arranged to transport "loyal klansmen and their families" to Rockford. At least one thousand Rockford men were to be inducted. A "tent city" was pitched just outside of the park grounds to accommodate ten thousand visitors (at a cost of fifty cents for a bed). A tent café seated five thousand people. American flags were to be posted along Auburn and North Main Streets to honor the pageant, but the KKK faced opposition.

The Klan Pageant Committee petitioned the Rockford City Council for the right to post the flags. The flags were to easily guide visiting pageant attendees to the driving park. Their proposal was submitted and simply signed, "Pageant Committee, Black Hawk Klan No. 76, Rockford, IL." After clerk Elmer O. Strand finished reading the petition during a city council meeting, alderman William F. Murphy asked, "What is the Black Hawk Klan?" Strand did not know. Murphy then replied, "I don't feel like voting on any petition unless the writer signs his name." Murphy motioned to table the petition. The aldermen unanimously tabled the pageant. Curious Rockfordians streamed through the park gates to see what was happening in the park. Citizens could drive around the track, since all of the construction was being completed in the infield. Klan officials were concerned that people would become injured if they ventured into the construction zone. Klan guards were posted at the gates to prevent "aliens" from trespassing.

Local newspaperman J. Howard Johnson petitioned the Rockford City Council meeting in person for American flags to be posted along the streets.

He petitioned not as a Klan member but as a publicity agent. He stated that no other organization had previously been denied a request such as the Klan's and that local officials were unwelcoming to thousands of visitors that were about to flood into Rockford. Alderman Murphy rose and motioned that the request be submitted to the Streets and Alleys Committee. Mayor J. Herman Hallstrom objected. Hallstrom alleged that the committee would take too long to decide. Hallstrom motioned for a vote. Murphy did not go down without a fight. The *Morning Star* recorded Murphy's opinion:

> *I have been for the Knights of Pythias, for the Masons, and for the Knights of Columbus, but I do not approve of any organization whose members are ashamed to show themselves. I went to Potro [sic] Rico in the Spanish-American War and I kept the American banner clean and brought it back in fine shape. The boys of '61 fought for the United States and they brought the flag back unsullied. We don't know who members of the Ku Klux Klan are. They won't march down the street with faces uncovered. We should not give them the right to handle Old Glory. They take the laws of the country into their own hands when they feel like it. You are satisfied with the laws. I am satisfied with the laws. They have threatened aldermen, clapping hands to their hips as if to draw a gun. They can't scare me. I've been threatened before. Let them throw off their hoods and come out like men and they can decorate the streets with American flags.*

One side of the council room erupted with applause. Other aldermen were not swayed. Alderman C. Henry Bloom rose and stated that as a member of the Labor Legion, he still favored the petition as signed, because he favored "free speech, free press, and free assembly." Alderman Jasper St. Angel rose and spoke about Klansmen arguing with him and mentioned that he had also been threatened with guns. St. Angel remarked,

> *They had guns with them. "We are going to hang American flags in the city regardless of whether the council grants our request" is what they said. They are going to take the law into their own hands. The Klan creates discrimination against people born in the old country. We are doing the best we can. The foreign element came here for a better living. It wants to keep on and it wants peace. This organization is against the laws of the United States. I am a law abiding American citizen, and will fight for America if I have to. The Ku Klux Klan should not receive permission to decorate streets with American flags.*

A vote was again called. Despite Murphy's and St. Angel's anti-Klan testimonies and two other aldermen joining their cause, the council voted in favor of posting the flags. Klansmen in the room cheered.

Other Klansmen met at Lyran Hall on Fourth Avenue at the same time as the city council meeting. The Klan meeting was restricted to the "Protestant public," and seven to eight hundred people attended. When news of the council's decision reached the Klan meeting, a great cheer rose from all that attended. The foremost KKK meeting speaker was sent by the Grand Dragon of the Illinois Realm, but his name was withheld from the newspapers. The meeting concluded with singing "Onward Christian Soldier," and a benediction was given by Reverend Charles A. Gage, pastor of the Centennial Methodist Church. Meanwhile, at the driving park, a Klansman in full regalia stood on the newly constructed platform, and two Klansmen, also in full regalia, patrolled the park gates. The Klan won against the city council and solidly controlled the driving park for the time being.

Stealthily, after midnight on September 6, Klansmen posted flags along State, Main and Fulton. Automobiles with flags attached to their hood ornaments, grills or headlights began to lumber into the city. The KKK event registration office was located at the Nelson Hotel. The Rockford-area hotels began to fill. Rockford Klansmen appealed to fellow resident Klansmen to rent out rooms to the visiting Klansmen.

Storm clouds threatened the September 7, 1923 event in the morning and dampened the track, but the rain held off in the afternoon. The Rockford Motorcycle Police enforced traffic. North Main Street north of Auburn Street and Latham Street was relegated to only northbound traffic. Automobiles from Illinois, Wisconsin and Michigan bounced down "bog-filled" Fulton Avenue. Huffman Boulevard was for southbound traffic only. Spectators arrived at the driving park gates at two o'clock and were greeted by two things. Pleasant music played from a large band, and they were physically searched by a Klansman. No liquor was permitted. Guns and cameras were confiscated but returned to their owners once they exited the park. Non-Klan members were welcomed along with their families. Admission to the pageant was seventy-five cents for men and fifty cents for women and children over twelve years of age. The festivities included numerous speeches, band concerts, evening fireworks and naturalization and induction ceremonies to end the day. The park gates closed at midnight on each of the two days.

Despite having to sit through a drizzle to see the first day's events, people came by the thousands. The *Republic* claimed that the event was attended by only eight thousand, because special trains that were to transport Klansmen from the surrounding states were unfilled. The Interurban Railway's regular service was adequate for the event days. The *Morning Star* claimed that the number of spectators swelled to between twenty and twenty-five thousand. Regardless of the exact number, the grandstands were filled. Hotdogs and barbecue were eaten. Concerts, solos, choirs and vaudeville acts were performed. The KKK's gigantic cross filled with red electric bulbs lit the night sky. However, not everything went to plan.

Dr. H.W. Evans, the Imperial Wizard, was unavailable. It was assumed that he was critically ill, because he had fainted giving a speech a few days earlier. Instead, one of his associates, "Daddy" DuBarr, made a speech in his place. The drizzling rain kept spectators cold and dampened ice cream sales. Some fireworks failed because rain dampened their powder. Live wires fell near the electrified cross, and people were warned to take care. There were not enough visitor tents provided for nightly sleeping quarters, and neither were they well received by the public. As spectators exited the park, they drove south on Huffman Boulevard. Suddenly, tires blew. Someone—or a group of people—had thrown a large number of tacks and nails onto the pavement. A total of 39 automobiles had all four tires blown and were completely disabled. Another 150 automobiles had either one or three tires blown. The newspapers lacked details about how motorists replaced their tires or how the disabled vehicles moved along Huffman, but it sent Klansmen a discouraging message.

On the second day, forty thousand people attended. Dr. Evans was still absent. Chicago's Reverend Elmer L. Williams, the "fighting parson," was invited to give a speech in his place. Approximately 1,500 people were initiated into the Klan, and a larger evening fireworks display was exploded, as well. The event was a success, and news of the Klan rally eventually faded. Soccer players took the places of Klansmen at the park.

The Rockford United soccer team changed their name to the Forest City soccer team. They were in a league with seven other Chicago teams and practiced as the Klansmen left town. The team's secretary, H. Heale, leased land just south of the park. Their first game was against the runner-up champion, Laburnum, of the Sons of Saint George League. The rough field slowed players considerably, but the game was enjoyed by three hundred spectators. In the first half, Rockford scored two goals and held the Chicago team to none. In the second half, the Rockford team appeared to be sluggish and allowed the Chicago team to score a goal but held them to only that one. The Forest Citys continued to win and were in a three-way tie for first place. With only two remaining games in the season, they were solely in first place with only one defeat. In the last game to end the first half of the season, the Rockford Forest Citys faced the undefeated Ivy White Rose. With the wind and sun at their backs, the Rockford team scored two goals in the first half and felt confident. However, conditions were unfavorable for the second half of the game, and the Ivy White Rose players managed to tie the game. Despite the tied game and their one-defeat record, the Rockford team had nothing about which to be ashamed. It was their first year in the league, and they played excellently against Chicago-area teams. In the meantime, the Swedish Gymnastic Club of Rockford challenged the Forest City soccer team to determine the stronger Rockford team. The clubs agreed to play three games. The Swedes played a very fast first game and won 2–1. The next game was to be played in Kishwaukee Park but was cancelled because both of the teams could not agree on a referee. Rockford was on top of the standings again at the beginning of 1924.

As 1923 came to an end, the park was once again vibrant with activity. The park served as a landing field for a Chicago eighteen-year-old pilot destined to a Dixon aerial show. John Huber built his own plane and flew into the driving park infield on November 11 to visit friends who lived on Melrose Street in Rockford. The Forest City soccer team was at the top of their league standings. Circuses intended to return. The Ku Klux Klan announced a five-year park lease. The group planned to construct a fifteen-thousand-person auditorium to hold enormous indoor meetings. The Needham bungalow within the park grounds was transformed into a clubroom. The Klan intended to have a strong permanent park presence for years to come, because the organizers hoped that "Klankraft Pageants" would become annual events. The park had reinvented itself into an open-air venue for the masses once again, allowing it to continue existing when many other driving parks constructed in the 1800s had completely disappeared.

14.

THINGS COULD GET UGLY

The Forest City Soccer Team continued to play in the park. The 1924 season opener was played against the Mistletoe Team from Chicago on May 4. The Mistletoe Team scheduled two train cars of one hundred fans to be brought into the city to watch the game. Defense ruled the day, as both teams remained scoreless after two halves. Rockford had two chances to score in the last minutes, but their shots were just wide. By mid-June, Rockford had competed with fiery toughness and was once again vying for first place in the St. George League. All they had to do was win against one more Chicago team at home on June 16. Rockford handled the Sunflowers with ease to win the league title. Meanwhile, Klan members met inside the driving park just north of where they played soccer and lit an oil-burning, thirty-one-foot-tall cross.

Rockford Driving Park was now a central headquarters for the Klan. Plans were already in progress for another large midwestern gathering during the Fourth of July holiday at the park. They also erected an electrified cross to replace the oil-burning one. Work on a huge grandstand that could seat ten thousand and concession areas also began in the park.

Details of the Midwest Conclave were announced in the *Republic* on the same day that the Forest City Eleven won the soccer league championship. Upwards of 100,000 Klansmen from Illinois, Wisconsin and Iowa were expected to travel to the area. They would fill hotels and local Klan members' homes and camp on the park grounds or around the park area. According to the *Republic*, "Imperial officers of national prominence, including Hiram W. Evans, imperial wizard, Atlanta, Ga., and S. Glenn Young, Williamson county federal agent and national Klan official, are on the speakers' program. The feature of the sessions will be the initiation of between 3,000 and 4,000 Klansmen in the second degree. A thousand candidates will be Winnebago county Klansmen, 128 of whom reside in Rockford, Mr. [Merle L.] Ward [who was the exalted cyclops of Blackhawk Klan No. 76 in Rockford] states." Other attractions, such as fireworks (which cost $3,500), a baseball game with another downstate Klan team (the Rockford Klansmen actually played against a Freeport team and won), a tribal dance group of Ojibwa Native Americans (ironically, but they did not perform), Zouave drill teams, bands from Chicago and Urbana, a replica of Stone Mountain built in the middle of the park and a downtown parade of Klansmen were in the planning stages. Klansmen placed small handbills on all the porches they could on the day before the conclave opened.

The Rockford police directed traffic toward the park. Automobiles were guided west down Fulton Avenue and could only exit the park south on Huffman Boulevard. Merle L. Ward expected more people to show up on the first day (July 3), and twenty-five thousand people came. Men and women were initiated as they looked upon the replica of Stone Mountain. Entertainment acts performed. Mrs. Park, a national leader for women in the KKK, gave a speech. Fireworks were set off at night.

On July 4, a Chicago band disembarked the train at the depot on Ninth Street. The KKK parade began there and wound its way through Rockford's downtown to John Street. Thousands crowded the parade route as Ward led on horseback. Robed, but with hoods up, Klansmen followed until they got into vehicles at John Street and made their way to the driving park. Buses from Milwaukee and Chicago made it to Rockford. More than 12,500 cars parked in the infield and around the park. According to Klan officials quoted in the *Republic*, a total of 80,000 people (30,000 more than the Klan's original expectations) came, and 961 new members were initiated into the Klan. More entertainment acts—such as comedians, Zouave drills, band concerts and vaudeville acts—were offered. On July 5, 10,000 people came to witness the closing ceremonies, including the initiations of women auxiliary members, foreign citizens becoming crusaders and young boys becoming junior knights. According to Klan authorities, a rough estimate between 100,000 and 125,000 people came to witness the activities over three days at the park. Plans were quickly made for another Klan meeting to be held August 6–8.

Not all Rockfordians believed that the Ku Klux Klan was great. Speeches were given by Illinois's Grand Dragon Charles G. Palmer and S. Glenn Young at the park. Palmer was a respected Chicago lawyer and wanted to maintain the KKK's respectful image since he believed that the Klan was close to controlling Illinois government officials, much like in Indiana. Young's personality was the opposite of Palmer's. Young was known for carrying weapons with him at all times. In southern Illinois, where Young originated, the KKK was strongly prohibitionist. Young performed liquor raids without the Klan's official permission. Young also became involved in numerous court cases and shootouts that provided negative publicity in opposition to the Klan's "family" image. However, Young had a strong following and was invited to speak at many Klan rallies. Since Young was a very controversial character, not everyone was pleased to hear him in Rockford. Rumors abounded about some Chicago men, or southern Illinois men, who were going to arrive in Rockford to assassinate Young. Special armed guards were placed at the driving park gates. According to the *Rockford Republic*, a group of four men tailed Young's high-powered vehicle all the way to Rochelle, where he stayed at a hotel surrounded by fellow Klansmen. The next morning, he was escorted by armed guards to the driving park and gave his speech. Supposedly, some of his guards spotted potential assassins around the speaker's platform, but none of them made a move. Once Young's speech was finished, he immediately left the park and returned home to Herrin, Illinois.

Most spectators enjoyed their time in the park. However, Ida Brady fell in the grandstand because the plank she was seated on gave way, and she fell several feet to the ground. Ten-year-old Viola Speake slipped and fell off the bleachers. As she fell, her ear was cut on one of the lower planks. Fannie Eisler experienced heart trouble while watching the proceedings at the park. Her condition improved the next day.

More entertainment at the park followed the day after the Klan's proceedings ended. On Sunday, July 6, the Roush and Carlisle Distributors of Star, Flint and Durant Automobiles in Rockford were to give an exhibition of their three-wheeled vehicles around the track. Jack Williams's aerobatics team was also to perform. Two planes, piloted by Melvin Cole and Homer Aavang, flew into the park. Williams was a wing-walker, and the other pilots could play "aerial polo" with toy balloons. The unique aspect of these exhibitions was the gate fee. It was free, but there was a collection taken for the flyers. The park continued to host numerous Blackhawk Klan baseball games throughout the rest of July. The club played against teams from Dekalb, Whig Hill and even the Rockford Cubs minor-league baseball team. The Klansmen were victorious until they played the Rockford Cubs and a team from Rockton that kept them scoreless, winning 10–0. In August, the Klan looked forward to another large three-day gathering.

A Klantauqua, much like a Chautauqua (which were generally held at Harlem Park), was planned for August 7–8. The event was open to all members and nonmembers and offered speakers on numerous Klan-approved topics. The traveling program appeared in Belvidere and in Freeport before it made its way to Rockford Driving Park. Merle L. Ward and Reverend LeRoy Mitchell were the chief planners who expected a crowd of two thousand people to attend. On August 7, only one thousand came. J.W. Correll, a legislator from Ohio, was the prominent speaker listed for August 8. According to the *Daily Register Gazette*, his speech was to be recorded and broadcast. To gain publicity for the event, another parade through Rockford's downtown was scheduled for the evening of August 8. No other information about the event could be found. The Klan continued to have meetings and continued to lease the driving park from Julius Graham but planned no additional events in the park until 1926, when the Klan Imperial Wizard was supposed to arrive and give a speech for another rally on October 4. In the interim, the KKK had approached Graham with a building proposal. The group wanted to build an auditorium or large meeting hall. Graham denied the request. The building projects may have interfered with all of the athletic activities that took place in the park.

In the meantime, the champion Forest City soccer team prepared to defend their title for the 1924–25 season. Season tickets sold at a decent rate. The majority of the championship players returned, and the new members showed promise. In early September, they played their first home game against the Milwaukee Acorns. They lost 0–1. They then played against the Rockford Swedish-American Gym team. That contest ended in a 3–3 tie. The two Rockford teams played against each other a week later and finished with another tie (1–1). Spectator numbers ranged between two and three thousand people. To raise funds for the team, improve field conditions and erect stands for fans, women associated with the team sold baked goods at Salamone's Market and held dances. By the end of the month, the Forest City team had won their first game against the Chicago Moss Rose team, and the Rockford Swedish-American Gym team was played and defeated by the Chicago team at the driving park. Enthusiasm for the game grew at such an alarming pace that Rockford Public School officials, along with those in Janesville, considered hiring a soccer coach to train high school teams. To encourage participation, one of the games was free for Rockford-area youth to attend.

By mid-October, N.L. Smith of the Rockford Area Chamber of Commerce had completed the first mail delivery night flight from Rockford to Chicago and back. Smith was a former air-mail pilot, and Jackie Howell, his business partner, was a Goodyear Rubber Company stunt pilot. A searchlight was installed on the driving park grounds, and wing flares on his plane guided Smith to his destinations. Not only was air-mail service thought about, but Smith and Howell also planned an air show for October 26. After the air show, hangers would be built. The park grounds were prepared for the show. Passenger service from the park never materialized, so perhaps mail service would prove more useful and successful. Airplanes had used the park throughout the 1920s, but nothing seemed permanent. "Hi Static," a local Rockford reporter, flew from Rockford Driving Park to the Trask Bridge Farmer's Picnic. However, just as Fred Spaulding had proposed aerial plans for the park, Smith must have gotten nowhere as well, because no reports about an air show appeared in the October 27 newspapers.

Things fell apart for the local soccer teams, too. The Forest City team was once again at the top of their league in the 1924 season. They challenged the Swedish Gym team for a third time. Arrangements were made, and Rockford teens were once again provided with free tickets to enjoy the game. The two teams had previously tied twice. Hopefully, this time, there would be a clear winner. On November 2, the two teams took to the field just south of the driving park where they always played. The game proved to be another nail-biter, because at the half, the teams remained tied. Frustration mounted. According to the Forest City team, their captain, Jack Lee, collided with a Swedish team player. Both players knocked themselves to the ground, but according to some Forest City fans, another Swedish player (or, according to the *Republic*, a Swedish fan) came up to Lee and purposely kicked him while he was still on the ground. Lee received a slash to the face that required stitches. Fans emptied onto the field, and for five minutes, a huge brawl between fans and players developed before officials brought it to an end. Referee George Anderson declared that the game was forfeited by both teams, and everyone was ordered to leave. Some Forest City fans were angry with Anderson because he had not called a fair game.

Two days later, the Swedish Gym team responded to these accusations in the *Republic*. According to them, the fight started because a Forest City player ran toward a Swedish player with his hands clenched and hit him. The fight between those two players was quickly broken up. The fans who rushed on to the field afterward were the ones who knocked Lee to the ground and kicked him in the face. As for the referee, Anderson was approved by the Forest City team and called the game to an end not because of the brawl but because the Forest City team refused to finish it. A. Anderson, who wrote the rebuttal in the *Republic*, ended his piece with questions: "Is it not a fact that all games which our team has played with other teams both here at home and in Chicago have been clean and friendly engagements? On the other hand, is there anyone who has seen a game in which the Forest City has engaged that did not end with violent arguments, threatening gestures and near-fights?" It was not expected that the two teams would meet again for the rest of the season.

At the end of November, the Forest City team was supposed to play the Chicago Laburnum team for the St. George League cup, but the Laburnum team cancelled the game. Due to financial difficulties or poor weather (newspaper accounts varied), the Laburnum team could not travel to Rockford. It was unlikely that the teams would be able to make up the game by the end of the year, so the Forest City team was left without the league's top honor. It wasn't until March 1925 that Laburnum's financial difficulties (or the weather) must have reversed, because the Forest City team played them then. Forest City lost 3–2 in the last fifteen minutes of the game. Their season continued on through April, but because of the loss, they could not win the title.

By June, a Texas-style roundup show was in town. Thirty performers and sixty head of livestock were once again destined for the park. Buffalos were brought in from North Dakota, and the main acts were Roman riding, steer and horse roping, horse jumping, relay races, comedy bucking mules and a clown rider. The newspapers did not report on the rodeo in Rockford, but other rodeos in other towns like Chicago were protested due to animal cruelty during the same months, so Rockford's humane society must have approved.

Athletics were once again in the spotlight by October 1925. A Rockford semi-professional football team played games at the driving park after the soccer team finished playing on Sunday afternoons. The Norwegian Athletic Club (NAC) football team's inaugural season was off to a good start at the driving park, too, because they had beat a Calumet team named the "Purple Triangles" and anticipated other tough-hitting Chicago-area semi-pro teams. However, as the soccer league progressed into 1926, the future looked grim, because Chicago teams began to cancel their game plans. The

Forest City manager complained bitterly to the St. George League officials because fans had appeared at Rockford Driving Park to witness contests, but no Forest City opponents appeared at the park. In another instance, Forest City had prepared to embark for Chicago in automobiles but were informed that the Chicago team they were to play planned to forfeit. No reasons were given for the cancellations, but it was suspected that finances were to blame. Rockford players and fans were upset, because soccer fervor was still high in this area. Soccer simply faded and gave way to another type of entertainment.

Rockford children of all ages were pleased to hear, as advance men came and posted fifty giant posters around town, that the Ringling Bros. and Barnum & Bailey Circus was to return to the Rockford Driving Park after two years. One of the headliners slated to appear in the Rockford show was May Wirth, who could somersault on horseback. The circus travelled to Rockford in four trains of one hundred railcars each that contained a complete herd of elephants, two hundred horses and a host of other exotic animals. Wirth was accompanied by one thousand other performers and crew members for the two shows. Attendance was expected to be high, because the National Guard was to begin exercises at Camp Grant during the same week. Soldiers would attend the circus while on leave. Despite not having a circus parade, people in Rockford noticed when they had arrived. Buses from Oregon and Byron brought people from the surrounding area to Rockford Driving Park on circus day. Even a thief wanted to attend the circus. A business in Freeport had been robbed overnight, and two circus tickets had been stolen—along with the business's cash—from the register.

The circus was a hit. Attendance soared to twenty-eight thousand. No injuries or accidents occurred. The acts were performed with excitement, and the audiences left feeling satisfied. Some even stayed to watch the circus load up and travel onward down the tracks toward Davenport. The only problem was the park's mud. Circus officials threw straw on the ground, but to no avail. Spectators' shoes became stuck. Automobiles were pulled out of the mud by circus draft horses. Once the cars were released, roads were jammed as spectators traveled home.

Before the park would become sleepy again for the winter, another Ku Klux Klan rally was planned for October 4. A crowd of thirty thousand was expected. A parade was scheduled to be led through the business district by KKK bands, juniors, Klanswomen, Tri-K girls and Krusaders from Chicago and Southern Wisconsin. They also led a march from the driving park gates south on Huffman Boulevard, east on Auburn Street, north on

"Hey! Skinnay"---
The Circus
Is Coming

THE HAGENBECK-
WALLACE CIRCUS

Will Exhibit In Rockford, at the Driving Park,
Friday, July 8

*The Clowns, Acrobats, Tigers,
Bareback Riders, Elephants,
Lions---All Will Be There.*

WANT TO GO FREE?

Any boy or girl living in Rockford can see this Wonderful Circus FREE as the guest of

THE ROCKFORD DAILY REPUBLIC

HOW YOU CAN GO TO THE
HAGENBECK-WALLACE CIRCUS

FREE!

Just get three persons who are not now subscribers of The Daily Republic to subscribe for The Daily Republic for 13 weeks at 15 cents a week.

You do not collect any money, the new subscriber pays the regular Republic carrier boy". All you have to do is be sure and see that none of the names of persons you send us are subscribers of The Republic at present, as none but new subscribers will count.

Important Notice!

Have all new subscribers sign their own name and address on the coupon. Send or bring the coupon below to The Rockford Daily Republic and receive your FREE pass to see America's foremost circus.

Clip This Blank—START TODAY!

USE THIS SUBSCRIPTION BLANK.

Rockford Daily Republic,
Rockford, Ill.

Please have The Rockford Daily Republic delivered to my residence (given below) for a period of thirteen weeks, for which I will pay every week my regular rate of 15 cents (15c) per week to The Rockford Daily Republic Carrier.

Signed .... Subscriber Must Sign Here.

Address ....

Town .... Apartment ....

Signed .... Subscriber Must Sign Here.

Address ....

Town .... Apartment ....

Signed .... Subscriber Must Sign Here.

Address ....

Town .... Apartment ....

Boy's Name ....

Address ....

Advertisement from *Rockford Republic*, June 29, 1927.

Main Street and west on Fulton Avenue to return to the park gates. The deputy Grand Dragon of Illinois, Chicago captain Scott E. Berridge, was also to give a speech. In reality, three to five hundred marched in the parade, and fifteen thousand spectators attended the rally in the park. Speeches were heard in the park past the midnight hour, but it is unclear as to who gave them, because journalists were purposely not informed. Local Blackhawk Klan members were elated at the turnout. The park became silent again for the rest of the fall and winter.

The park was clear of snow and remained quiet until another circus was slated to come to town. On July 8, 1927, the Hagenbeck-Wallace Circus was to perform two shows in one day at the park. The main attraction was the opening number, "The Geisha," which included 1,000 performers, 200 circus animals, 750 horses and 25 elephants. The closing number, called "Blazing Glory" (or "Glittering Glory"), included the same number of performers. The circus trains pulled onto a siding near the park grounds early in the morning.

Fred Pagel and his wife arrived at the park to watch the circus unload only to have their automobile stolen by Booker T. James off of Lawndale Street. Just as the circus left town, circus worker William Humphrey stole $1,000 of merchandise from the North Side Cleaning Company. The thefts were both allegedly committed by African American males. The Robertson Theater Company held performances at the park in August. In the *Daily Register Gazette*, the company stated that it only employed the best people. No doubt the company realized what had occurred at the park during and after the circus had left. The park's reputation was still intact for hosting a great variety of spectacles.

15

CURTAIN CALLS

$\mathcal{E}$d F. O'Connor had been part of the park's history since it was founded in 1891. He was a former vice president of the driving park association and trained horses there for many years. In early September 1927, O'Connor was a judge for the Ogle County Fair harness races. While off the track, O'Connor was a realtor and made loans. On September 28, 1927, O'Connor left his office around 10:00 a.m. He told his secretary that he was "going out for a while" and "would be back before noon." His secretary, Miss Philipp, thought that he was in good spirits on that morning. When he left his office, he could not find where he parked his car. For a half-hour, he looked, and finally he located it. He then went to the Burr Sporting Goods store and bought a .38-caliber handgun. Afterward, he drove his Ford coupe to the driving park and parked his car facing north, on the west side, in the quarter stretch of the track. O'Connor must have sat there and thought of all of the "good old days" of racing, the bell-ringing, crowds cheering, cigars smoked, bets made and the sounds of beating hooves on the track. All was gone. No horses had raced on the track in years, and weeds grew through it everywhere. He raised the gun to his right temple, pulled the trigger and slumped over the left side of his seat.

J.E. Aue was the park caretaker and saw a car pull into the park. He assumed the driver had a girl with him and noticed the parked automobile between 1:30 and 1:45 p.m. He was irritated, because automobiles frequently came into the park without permission. He approached the car and found that this was not an ordinary trespasser. He immediately notified the sheriff's department. Deputies Harold Baker and Fletcher Crawford were the first to arrive. Fred C. Olson took the body into his care and then visited the O'Connor home, where he broke the news to Mrs. O'Connor. A note tacked on the steering wheel of the coupe or left on the seat (newspaper reports varied) read, "Dear Mother [his wife], Don't blame me for this. I was driven to it. I love my family so much I can't help it. Pray for me and have the children take care of you. PAPA." Financial reverses and failing health (Alzheimer's or dementia) may have been the reasoning behind his actions. He was fifty-five years old, and the park had been part of his life for over half of his lifetime.

By 1928, the park had served the community for thirty-eight years, but once again, it showed its age. George Gough lived close to the driving park on Carney Avenue. In March, he was accused of stealing wire from the driving park house. The house had no tenant (the KKK must have moved on) and had been vandalized so badly that it needed $3,000 in repairs. The case against Gough was delayed due to a lack of evidence. There were no other suspects mentioned, and it is unlikely that anyone was officially charged.

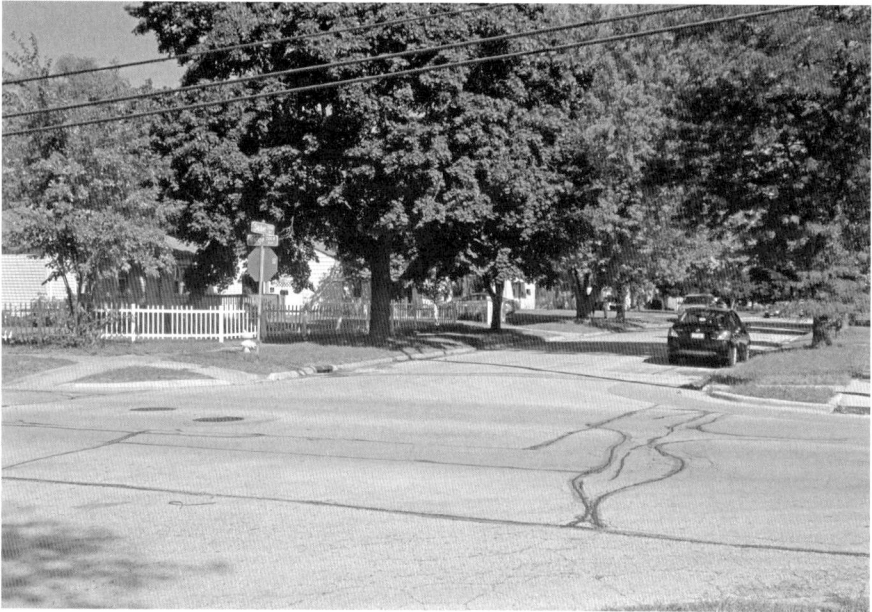

The intersection of Ridge Avenue and Sauber Avenue where the northwest turn was located and where Ed O'Connor committed suicide. *Photograph by the author.*

140

On April 15, 1928, the park's illustrious owner, Julius Graham, died. Julius Graham was the last surviving son of Freemon Graham, and Julius's wife, Emily Brantingham Graham, had died in 1922. His daughter Edith Needham and her husband, Henry, had controlled the park for years before his passing. Graham was involved in many things other than the park. He was a business partner in his brothers' distillery, owned a cotton factory on South Main Street and a match factory (he later sold to Diamond Match Company, and it burned down afterward) and had served as an alderman for the fifth ward. Graham was eighty-three years old, and like Ed O'Connor, the park would have been part of his life for almost half of his lifetime, too.

The newspapers began to wonder if even the circuses would choose to hold their spectacles at a location off of Harrison Avenue. Perhaps the park had lost its appeal because there was nothing attractive about it. In May, the Robbins Circus pulled into town and promised to feed one thousand people by cooking on their huge ranges. The *Republic* believed that the circus was a great way for children to learn about animals in person instead of from books. When the circus arrived in Rockford, it was an hour late. The circus parade, which was planned for both sides of the river, was shortened. Hundreds of children of all ages on the east side of the river hustled over to the west side to see it. The circus boasted one hundred acts with three hundred performers. The crowds came as fields around the park filled with automobiles. The circus manager believed that the circus would return to Rockford the following year.

Even before they performed, the Sells Floto Circus advertised in the *Morning Star* for the July 9 circus. On July 9, the Sells Floto Circus arrived late in Rockford. The scheduled parade was canceled because the workers needed time to set up the tents for the show. The Rockford police station was bombarded by calls from children asking about the parade—but it would not be happening. Ten-year-old Eldridge Davis was extremely excited to finally see some of the circus cars near his home on Sixteenth Street. He thought that he could jump onto the train, but he failed. His grip loosened on the side rail, and he fell underneath the train. Only his foot was crushed, and his mother accompanied him in the police ambulance to Swedish-American Hospital, where his foot was amputated. The circus train never stopped, because no one noticed what had happened.

From nine in the morning until noon, circus workers quickly raised tents. One of the performers was very familiar with the Rockford area. Irene Ledgett (née Hill) was a horsewoman and elephant trainer who grew up in Rockford. She originally wanted to be a journalist after graduating from Rockford High School. While covering a circus in Ohio, she rode an elephant and was immediately enthralled. She quit her job at the newspaper and ran away with the circus.

Fred Ledgett was also from Rockford and became interested in the big top after seeing the W.B. Reynolds Show at Fairgrounds Park in 1892. He ran away from home at age fifteen to join the circus as a bareback rider and never looked back. Ledgett worked his way up the ranks and became the lead horse trainer in the Sells Floto Circus and in many other circuses during his career. Irene and Fred were married in 1922. The couple's first return to Rockford was in 1925, when the Sells Floto Circus performed in July off of Harrison Street. The Ledgetts made many return visits to Rockford as performers and, after the circus seasons had concluded, to reside.

Over two hundred children from local area agencies were invited to see the Sells Floto Circus free of charge thanks to local charities. After the eight o'clock evening performance concluded, the circus train began traveling down the tracks to the next stop at one in the morning. The driving park would not be without clowns, animals and sideshows for very long. The Ringling Bros. and Barnum & Bailey Circus came on July 30. The circus arrived in four special circus trains and unloaded thousands of animals and performers. The circus was so large that no circus parade was needed through the streets of any city. When the circus was finished setting up, there were thirty-two tents (the main one was seven hundred feet long). The shows were filled to capacity, with twenty thousand people attending them (ten thousand per show). Seven rings of entertainment made it difficult to judge where to look. There was a nine-hundred-pound sea lion, acrobats, clowns, shows and more, and once the shows were over, the tents came down and the four circus trains vanished. A *Republic* journalist stated it best:

> *The circus has gone for a year, but long after the stalks of tall grass in the driving park, flattened by a myriad* [of] *human and animal feet, have become once more erect and after winds and rain have destroyed the last evidence of the post holes and wagon ruts—long after that the circus will still be here and alive in hundreds and hundreds of young hearts—and many older ones too.*

The only unfortunate event that occurred while the circus was in town was when seven-year-old William Orlando was caught between two buses on Huffman Boulevard while returning home after the evening performance. He was examined at the hospital and only suffered minor bruises.

The weeds and grasses of Rockford Driving Park did manage to regain their stature. Property owners along Rockton Avenue and Huffman Boulevard were abuzz over extending the roadways northward in late 1928. Huffman was to be extended to the Eddy Farm boundaries, and Rockton was to follow the railroad tracks all the way to North Main Street near Halstead. The city was going to be extended northward, and it made sense to plan for the future, but the plans remained just plans for the time being.

The end of the decade was approaching. In the beginning months of 1929, advertisements appeared that read: "Ten old cars wanted. Will pay cash. Driving Park Forest 5633." By May, the advertisements had changed to: "Used car parts for sale. Repairing. Also used cars bought and sold." No name was associated with the advertisements. The park was too large to simply turn into a car lot. Plans were underway for another circus season, but with a motor-oil twist.

The Robbins Brothers Circus made plans in April 1929 to arrive for another show at the park on May 19. The opening theme was "Mother Goose and Santa Claus in Fairyland," and the closing performance was a salute to U.S. history that included fifty Sioux Native Americans, cowboys and hundreds of other performers. Two special trains arrived to transport five elephant herds and the world's largest hippopotamus, Miss Iowa, and the world's largest elephant, Big Bingo. In addition to that show, a two-mile-long circus parade wound through both the east and west Rockford downtown business districts. Despite the rainy skies, people lined the streets to see it. Children appeared on the driving park grounds to bring water for the elephants once the parade was over. It is interesting to note that both white and African American children were seen working together despite the presence of the Ku Klux Klan in the park just a few years before.

In addition to animals and performers, a car show was supposed to entice new spectators to come through the gates. D.R.F. Chevrolet, a local dealer, decided to dedicate an entire tent to displaying the latest six-cylinder automobiles and trucks. The Robbins Brothers believed that the car show was one of the greatest additions to their show.

A month later, another circus came to the driving park. The John Robinson Circus had been entertaining people since 1842. Those who could prove that they had seen a show at least fifty years ago were admitted free of charge. This circus boasted that it had the largest hippo in the world, Victor, as well as the tiniest hippo, Tinymite. The circus management had changed all of its acts from the previous year and included performers from around the world, including nine Arab riders. Though the show was smaller than the Robbins Brothers Circus, Rockfordians enjoyed it by the hundreds. So many circuses performed at the driving park that the park begun to sport the title "Driving Park Circus Grounds" in several advertisements. However, Robinson's circus was the last to visit the park in 1929. Another type of attraction was headed its way in early September.

The Rubin and Cherry Model Shows leased the driving park from September 9 to September 14, 1929. A three-thousand-foot-long canvas fence was erected around the entire grounds. This outfit had absolutely everything. It included a Wild West show, midget circus, Hawaiian troubadours, kid shows, a motordrome for a rip-riding motorcycle, magicians, a colored troupe of entertainers and minstrels, auto races driven by monkeys and carnival rides. They employed forty local people to simply sell tickets on the grounds.

However, the show did not go on as planned. Before the Wild West show and midget circus even unfurled their tents, an agent for the state's attorney appeared on the park grounds. He ordered the two outfits to not perform because carnival companies could not exhibit in the state, according to the law, unless they were performing at a county fair or by permission of a county board. The attorney for Rubin and Cherry believed that they were not a carnival but an entertainment organization, because they had no concession stands or "grafting attachments." It was quickly realized that by the time the lawyers would have their day in court, the engagement in Rockford would be over. Rubin and Cherry complied with the complaint and shipped their Wild West show and midget circus down the rail lines toward South Carolina before the rest of the group left Rockford. The organization charged a ten-cent gate fee and believed that they were no different from the two circus outfits that had performed in Rockford in the previous months. A competitor who had been turned down for an entertainment lease between the previous circuses and Rubin and Cherry's engagement was believed to have gone to the state's attorney's office and filed a complaint against Rubin and Cherry. Rubin and Cherry claimed to have lost money due to the cancelation of their shows and vowed to return for another engagement the following year outside the Rockford city limits.

Despite the market reports in late 1929, in 1930, the Clarence A. Wortham World's Best Show, presented by the Rockford Central Labor Union, opened just south of the driving park (now known as Huffman Park). The Wortham organization included a variety of acts, sideshows and carnival rides. An electric generator lit the attractions at night. The children attending the newly built Welsh Elementary School had trouble concentrating as the show rolled into town in late May. The crowds came in droves despite the cool weather and light showers. Show management was happy about the rain, because it kept down the dust. Otherwise, they would have had to use their sprinkler wagons.

Once the shows left, Rockford Driving Park was to return to its roots by thrilling spectators in a way it used to. It is interesting to note that the Wortham shows were set up outside of the driving park gates and not located inside of the park. The exact reasoning for this is unclear, but it may have been due to some discussions held at the Faust Hotel between the Walter R. Craig American Legion Post and "Speed" Bradford. Bradford owned a Cord 6 automobile and wanted to break the national and international record for the fastest five-hundred-mile dirt-track time. To achieve his goal, a never-attempted stunt of racing an airplane near his automobile to refuel it would have to be achieved. Bradford leased the driving park for June 29, 1930, and Winnebago County graders were brought into the park to restore the original mile track into racing shape. The track had not been used for racing for almost a decade and had disappeared underneath the grass. All of

Death Curve At Driving Park

"Speed" Bradford inspects the Rockford Driving park track which is being put in condition by county highway department workers for the famous racer's 500-mile grind in the powerful Cord front-drive roadster shown in the picture. Mud-holes and tall grass will be turned into one of the fastest tracks in the state before the race against time, which will be held a week from next Sunday at the north side park. Proceeds from the race are to be used for sending the Walter R. Craig post, American Legion, drum and bugle corps to the annual Legion convention in Boston, Mass.

"Speed" Bradford stands in front of his Cord automobile at Rockford Driving Park. *From "Death Curve at Driving Park," Republic, June 19, 1930.*

the proceeds from Bradford's time trial would be given to the Walter Craig American Legion Post's Drum and Bugle Corps in Rockford so that they could attend a national competition in Boston.

Bradford had an interesting background. In his last year of university on the East Coast, he decided to do something unique with his life. He made arrangements with a publisher to walk backward from New York, New York, to Seattle, Washington. When he arrived in New York, the publisher backed out of the deal. Undeterred, Bradford sold all of his belongings and completed the trip anyway. His next feat was to ride a bicycle across the country, but he failed after an accident. Soon, automobile endurance racing enticed his interests.

His 1930 Rockford Driving Park appearance was not the first time he was in Rockford. In 1927, he planned to make the fastest time between Des Moines, Iowa, and Chicago. Rockford was one of his planned stops. He had only five minutes to stop in front of the newspaper office and distribute fifty new pennies. When he arrived, only two minutes off of his expected time, his car was surrounded by waiting people. Once he left, a board in front of the newspaper office kept track of his progress along his route.

Excitement returned to the park in a new form. Once the track had been readied, other preparations were made, such as building a bridge across the track to allow spectators to cross the track during the race. Spectators could watch the action from the infield and eat from food stands, since there was no longer a grandstand at the park. Spectators, food stands and automobiles were not the only things found in the infield. A sixty-foot-wide runway for airplanes was also constructed for the refueling plane. Fred Machesney flew around the Rockford area and dropped hundreds of handbills promoting the event, because the refueling pilot worked for him. Bradford also promoted his stunt when he appeared at the Palace Theater shows. He prepared his Cord Roadster by stripping everything (fenders, headlights, spare tire and such) off of it to make it faster. The nation was taking notice of his plans. It was announced in late June that Pathé News would send a film crew to Rockford to film the midair refueling process.

The forecast for the day was for clouds. If the sun had beaten down, Bradford may have experienced a tire blowout due to high heat and the demand put on his vehicle. The crowds descended on the park. Bradford had practiced many laps in the previous weeks leading up to this day. The event began at 9:00 a.m. Al St. John piloted the refueling plane, Jack Hugg was Bradford's relief driver and L.F. Wiley was Bradford's mechanic in charge of grabbing the hose to refuel the Cord Roadster. As the Curtiss airplane

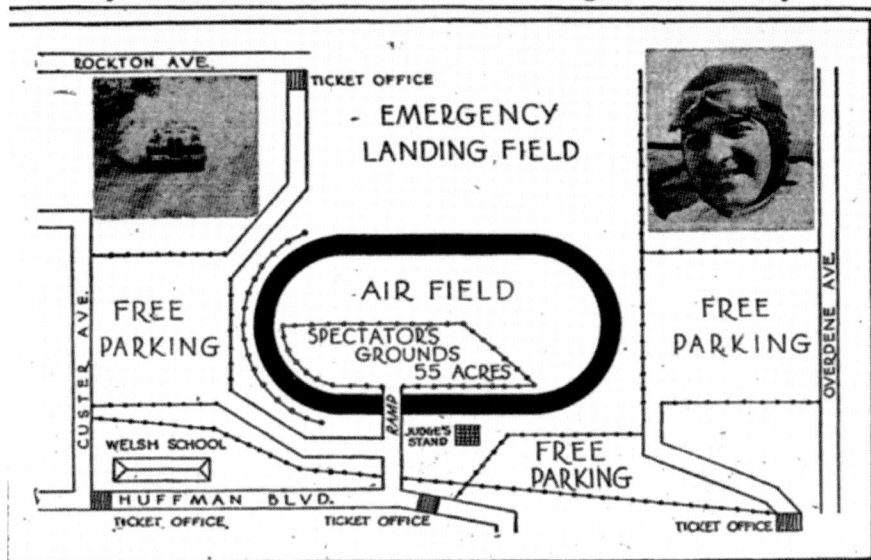

Driving park map from the day "Speed" Bradford tried to break the speed record. *From "Map Shows How to Get to American Legion Race Today," Republic, June 29, 1930.*

flew over the automobile, the connection was not made. By lap 230 of 500, Bradford decided to let Hugg take the wheel. Hugg rounded the track for an hour before he let Wiley take over for him. Wiley was unable to push the last half of the five hundred miles, so the endurance race ended short of its goal. The newspapers were mostly silent about the affair.

Positively, local drivers realized that they now had a new track on which they could again race machines. Beuford "Doc" Shanebrook was the son of an optometrist and had raced in Chicago during the late 1920s. He believed that he could achieve Bradford's goal, but he also failed in his attempt. Undeterred, Shanebrook promoted new races for local automobile drivers and motorcyclists at Rockford Driving Park for one day in July and one day in August. If the races were successful, Shanebrook planned to build a new grandstand and a board track needed for racing. Shanebrook's plans never came to fruition. If races were held on August 10, 1930, they were the last motorized races that the park would ever host. A large amount of effort was put into refurbishing the track, but the economics of the time kept people away.

16.

SHADOWS AND DUST

Rockford was like thousands of cities across the country during the Great Depression. Workers lost their jobs, factories closed, wages were cut and savings were lost. Investors and spectators simply did not have disposable money to spend on extravagant things like racing. People were more likely to sell their automobiles than race them. Edith Needham, the owner of Rockford Driving Park, knew this. She also had to pay property taxes on the park. Granted, many shows came to the park, such as the Barnum & Bailey Circus, but it was not enough to justify the continuous possession of the park. On April 23, 1931, the *Register-Republic* announced that Edith Needham had sold the park to the Rockford Realty Company. The eighty-acre tract was divided into 373 residential lots, and the subdivision later extended to Halsted Road. This sale was not unusual. Around the country, many small racetracks disappeared and became residential areas. Harlem Park closed in 1928 and was also plotted as a subdivision. The subdivision plans were made, but they were far from reality. Buyers could not afford to build new houses on the lots of both parks, so the land remained vacant. This allowed the driving park to continue hosting events despite its sealed fate.

The track quickly became a memory as the land reverted to simply being a giant field. Rockford Driving Park, in its final stages, became like its greater competitor, the family-oriented Harlem Park. Its transformation from racetrack to temporary traveling-family theme park allowed the park to survive throughout most of the 1930s, when other parks struggled. The

The lots and streets were drawn over the original. *From* Atlas of the City of Rockford and Vicinity, *Th. L. Leon de Tissandier.*

Veterans of Foreign Wars (VFW) planned a carnival at Rockford Driving Park for its annual state gathering. Land directly south of the park (now known as Huffman Park) was reserved for it. The show went on, in contrast to the thousands of national permanent amusement parks that closed their gates between 1910 and 1933. Thousands of local children came to enjoy the rides for the reduced price of five cents. In fact, throughout the rest of 1931 to 1933, circus after circus arrived in the park. Many of the attractions were similar, with most featuring elephants, trained monkeys and displays of horsemanship. Each show and circus left town with profits in hand as children from Rockford and surrounding areas packed the attractions. Many Rockford children of the 1930s saw the park as the "circus grounds" instead of a racetrack. Rockford parents could find the pocket change to attend the circus, and for a moment, economic woes were forgotten and all was wonderful in the world for parents and children alike.

Before the park's final closing, there was one more controversy. Edith Needham was upset with city officials because she believed that they had taken more of her land than was agreed upon for the paving of Huffman Boulevard. Needham still held the property west of Huffman between Fulton Avenue and Brown Street and presented the city with a bill for $500. According to the *Register-Republic*, "Members of the council contended that the improvement

149

to Mrs. Needham's property was greater than the value of the property the city had appropriated for street purposes." Needham rebuked the council and believed that her property received no such benefit. In fact, Needham may have been correct. In 1929, the council approved a plat for subdividing driving park, which showed that the disputed strip of land was indeed still owned by Needham. However, the plat was never officially recorded. By August 1935, the council had officially voted in favor of taking no action on Needham's threat to sue the city for $500. Needham did not follow through on her threat, because no other legal action was taken.

On July 12, 1936, an advertisement that appeared in the *Morning Star* read: "New house. Three rooms and a bath. Private owner. Location one block northwest of Huffman and Fulton in Driving Park." It was the first home to be built in the park since the Needhams built their home there in 1912. The economic outlook and building plans around the park continued to brighten through the next year. The Winnebago County Highway Department sought a six-acre tract of land just east of the park to build new machine shops, garages and offices for the department. Unfortunately, the plans called for spending $50,000, and the budget was $7,000 short. In addition, the Rockford Board of Education raised concern because of its proximity to Welsh Elementary School. However, despite the board's concerns and that of other highway department board members, sealed bids on the proposed new site were quickly collected from five Rockford area contractors (all of which were rejected, because they were all believed to be too high).

The circuses also sensed a change. The Ringling Bros. and Barnum & Bailey Circus leased a tract of land off Harrison Avenue and Eighth Street

Huffman Boulevard is a boulevard due to the centrally located streetcar tracks. Huffman ceases to be a boulevard at Fulton Avenue's park gates. *Photograph by the author.*

for their performance in July 1937 instead of renting the driving park. The *Morning Star* reported that "a decision to hold the circus at the Harrison avenue [*sic*] grounds instead of the driving park was reached after north end residents owning building lots in the vicinity objected to the presence of the circus in their neighborhood last year." Other circuses followed suit. The Beckmann and Gerrety Carnival was granted permission to host its entertainments at the Buckbee property on Seminary Street and Fifteenth Avenue instead of at Rockford Driving Park.

The final circus to perform at the driving park was the Sells-Sterling Circus on May 21, 1938, for one day only. Instead of arriving in railcars as previous circuses had, the company arrived in "56 new all-steel semi-trailer trucks." Instead of hoisting the tents using elephants and manpower, "modern mechanical devices, operated by steam and electric power" were used. Once their trucks were packed and drove away from the grounds, the Rockford Driving Park ceased to act as a public park. No more crowds would come to see horses, bicycles, runners, shooting matches, motorcycles, automobiles, Great War reenactments, rodeos, aerial stunts, county fairs, KKK rallies or circuses. The park's fate was like that of many driving parks across the nation.

The park took on a new life, this time for good, as the Driving Park Subdivision took shape. On June 6, 1939, a petition was filed in the Winnebago County clerk's office to officially annex a majority of the driving park into the city of Rockford. The petition was accepted by the end of the month. Water mains were extended to the area in 1941, and sewer systems were extended in the mid-1940s. On October 12, 1952, the *Register-Republic* reported:

> *Low-priced prefabricated ranch homes are being completed at a rate of four a week in a unique building program underway in the old Driving Park in northwest Rockford....So far, about 55 of these two and three-bedroom homes have been completed and at least 40 of them are occupied. The homes are built upon order. Barnes and Sjostrom have purchased 80 lots in the subdivision for erection of new homes on Ridge ave., Huffman blvd., Sauber ave., Glenwood ave., and Overdene ave. A model home is located at 1928 Sauber ave....Barnes said a three-bedroom ranch home with utility room sells for $10,400...a two-bedroom homes sells for $9,750. Barnes said the National Homes Corporation, the biggest manufacturer of prefabricated houses in the country, has built 47,000 homes for distribution throughout the nation. At present a buyer has a choice of 28 different floor plans.*

Starting after World War II, prefabricated homes were constructed en masse across the United States and Europe. Wartime assembly-line production led to the development of thousands of products. In the postwar years, there was a housing shortage, which created a bigger demand for homes to be built quickly. Kit homes, such as the ones sold by Sears in the early 1900s, were no longer sold after the 1940s due to the Great Depression and wartime production needs. Kit homes also required more labor than prefabricated ones, which could be fully constructed in days. By the early 1960s, the Indiana-based National Homes Corporation had built 250,000 prefabricated homes across the country. The advantage of a prefabricated home over a traditionally built home was that the materials were cheaper (thinner studs and plywood roofs) and required less-skilled tradesmen. Some of those homes can still be found in the Driving Park Subdivision today.

By 1938, the park had served the Rockford community for forty-eight years. Times had dramatically changed since the field was first planted with bushes and trees as a nursery, then later plowed before the first horse and driver stepped onto the track. In 1916, George Burnap was the landscape architect of Washington, D.C. In his book *Parks: Their Design, Equipment and Use*, he wrote about driving parks across the country:

> *Many recreation parks, because of their extensive areas and naturalistic character, often become known as Driving Parks, a suppositional pleasure of the rich or of the comparative few who may have carriages and automobiles. Such parks, if actually exclusive, are a burden on any city, contributing to the enjoyment of too small a minority to justify their expense and maintenance. They should be immediately taken in hand, and arranged or rearranged to serve a larger purpose. Every expedient of design should be called upon and be made use of to convert each into a recreation ground for all, affording everyone opportunities of outdoor pleasure and enjoyment of a sort that will win general appreciation and approbation.*

Burnap's analysis summarizes, in large part, the history of Rockford's Driving Park, because from its onset, the park became a struggle for the businessmen who created it, too few people attended its various racing meets, yet the park was repeatedly repurposed and survived longer than many other driving parks across the country because of its transformative nature. The park weathered many storms and remained open to the public despite its private ownership. There was something lasting to it. Since it was mostly an open field, it could continually reinvent itself, unlike many other permanent

Right: Advertisement from *Morning Star*, April 2, 1939.

Below: *From left to right*: Bengt Sjostrom, Carl Fradine and Charles E. Barnes. *From "Finish Prefabs at Rapid Rate,"* Register-Republic, *October 11, 1952.*

New Homes for Old Driving Park

Adolphson Road formed a small southeastern section of the track. *Photograph by the author.*

entertainment venues. At the time, Rockford citizens shared greatly varied memories of the park. Some remembered the park for its horse racing; some for its motorcycle and automobile racing. Others may have remembered the high school track meets or the soccer games, the rodeo roundups, the circuses or perhaps the KKK rallies. It was remembered not only by those who attended events there but also by those who just played in its mud, like Lloyd Fry did as a kid. But once the weeds grew thicker and the subdivision construction crews came, the park disappeared from maps, and memories faded.

As Rockford Driving Park became a subdivision, the Deery family built its replacement. The Rockford Speedway was built in 1948, only ten years after the last event was held at Rockford Driving Park. The speedway was built far away from subdivisions and was developed for the sole purpose of racing stock cars. Today, the speedway faces challenges to those the driving park did almost a century ago. Subdivisions are being built around it. Other venues of entertainment draw away crowds. Racing does not appeal to everyone. To stay profitable, the speedway has adapted to other purposes, such as hosting the Rockford Carnival, just like the driving

Right: The area between Adolphson Road and the railroad track near the Rockford Driving Park gate was where the small depot was located. *Photograph by the author.*

Below: The intersection of Ridge and Bell Avenues is where the start/finish line was located. *Photograph by the author.*

155

park once did. The speedway has also hosted nationally recognized drivers and entertained crowds for seventy years and continues to entertain. No one knows whether the speedway will eventually share the same fate as the Rockford Driving Park.

None of the historical monographs of the city's history contain major references to the park or its vivid history. Fairgrounds Park is remembered. Harlem Park and Central Park are remembered. Rockford Driving Park is forgotten. The driving park did not have a continuous history due to its on-again, off-again nature, while the other parks and fairgrounds did. Rockford Driving Park was located on the outskirts of town on the northwest side with limited transportation options to deliver people to the park. The other parks had more transportation options, and the fairgrounds were located close to the downtown area. Rockford Driving Park involved racing, which not everyone was excited about, and this was its original exclusive purpose. The other amusement parks were family-oriented, but Rockford Driving Park started as an exclusively built gentleman's racetrack complete with a reputation for alcohol and gambling. The other parks continuously provided a variety of attractions. Rockford Driving Park left no solid historical record—hardly any pamphlets, pictures or books, and no physical structures (fences, barns, gates, stands) remain in existence. Harlem Park's images are preserved in hundreds of postcards, Central Park is preserved by pictures and advertisements and the fairgrounds are remembered due to its preservation as a park today. The erasure of the Rockford Driving Park's history is a mystery.

However, traces of the park remain today. The private residence of the Needhams still exists. The subdivision that was built on the grounds is known as the "Driving Park Subdivision." Huffman Boulevard is still a boulevard because of the streetcar that took passengers to the park's main gate at Fulton and Huffman. This explains why the boulevard ends there. Bell Avenue is, in all likelihood, named after the finish line that once was located at the intersection of Bell and Ridge Avenues. However, these are simply shades of what was once a prime attraction on the outskirts of the Rockford city limits that are not easily discernable to the average Rockford citizen.

There are many structures being built in the city today to attract people to the Rockford area. Sports tourism is the new term for a very old idea. Instead of the sounds of hoofbeats and engines filling hotel rooms and restaurants, now it is the sound of whistles, soccer balls and basketballs that fill them instead. It is unknown if these new sports complexes will be remembered or forgotten like the shadows and hoofprints of Rockford's Driving Park.

BIBLIOGRAPHY

Atlas of the City of Rockford and Vicinity. Th. L. Leon de Tissandier, 1917.

Burnap, George. *Parks: Their Design, Equipment and Use.* Philadelphia, PA: J.B. Lippincott Co., 1916.

"Charles 'Fearless' Balke." The First Super Speedway, Mark Dill Enterprises, Inc. Accessed July 5, 2014. http://www.firstsuperspeedway.com/photo-gallery/charles-fearless-balke.

Cline, Bruce L., and Lisa A. Cline. *History, Mystery, and Hauntings of Southern Illinois.* Rockford, IL: Black Oak Media Inc., 2011.

Connors, Tiffany. "How Prefab Houses Work." How Stuff Works. Accessed July 23, 2017. https://home.howstuffworks.com/prefab-house1.htm.

Cunningham, Pat. "Pat's Stuff." *Rockford Register Star,* August 4, 2004.

DeBock, Michael. "Vintage Indian/Harley Moto…: With a Splash of Cars and Women Album." Accessed November 16, 2014. https://www.flickr.com/photos/mdebock/albums/72157636265070875.

Figy, James. "Hoosier-made Prefab Homes Pose Unique Problems." Angie's List. Accessed July 23, 2017. https://www.angieslist.com/articles/hoosier-made-prefab-homes-pose-unique-problems.htm.

Grand Encampment of Knights Templar. Accessed February 2, 2015. www.knightstemplar.org.

"History of the Excelsior Henderson, the Road to Glory." Accessed June 30, 2014. http://www.reocities.com/don4bigrig98/.

Holland and Ferguson & Company. Title Abstract for Lot 25, Block 7 Driving Park Subdivision.

Kersh, Steve. "Big Builder Getting It Together Again." *Chicago Tribune*, July 26, 1987. Accessed July 23, 2017. http://articles.chicagotribune.com/1987-07-26/business/8702240616_1_houses-national-homes-hampton-park.

"The Ku Klux Klan in Williamson County, Part Two." Marion, Illinois History Preservation. Accessed June 10, 2015. http://www.mihp.org/2013/09/the-ku-klux-klan-in-williamson-county-part-two/#/.

"Leslie Allen." Old Racing Cars. Accessed July 5, 2014. http://www.oldracingcars.com/driver/Leslie_Allen.

McShane, Clay, and Joel A. Tarr. *The Horse in the City: Living Machines in the Nineteenth Century*. Baltimore, MD: Johns Hopkins University Press, 2007.

Mozer, David. "Chronology of the Growth of Bicycling and the Development of Bicycle Technology." International Bicycle Fund. Accessed July 12, 2016. http://www.ibike.org/library/history-timeline.htm.

National Amusement Park Historical Association. "Great Moments." Accessed July 15, 2017. http://www.napha.org/LIBRARYRESOURCES/FactsFigures/GreatMoments/tabid/69/Default.aspx.

Needham, Harry Stainthrope. "World War I Draft Card." National Archives.

Norton, Richard Arthur. "John Lawson." http://www.findagrave.com/cgi-bin/fg.cgi?page=gr&GRid=119923584.

Portrait and Biographical of Winnebago and Boone Counties, IL. Chicago, IL: Biographical Publishing Company, 1892.

"Real Road Racing." Harold Osmer Publishing. Accessed July 5, 2014. http://www.hopublishing.com/real-road-racing.html.

Rockford (IL) Daily-Register Gazette.

Rockford (IL) Daily Spectator, 1893.

Rockford (IL) Morning Star.

Rockford (IL) Republic.

"The Standardbred." Equiworld. Accessed February 25, 2013. http://www.equiworld.net/breeds/standardbred/index.htm.

Statnekov, Daniel K. "Pioneers of American Motorcycle Racing." Accessed July 5, 2014. http://www.statnekov.com/motorcycles/lives12.html.

Temple, Robert. *The History of Harness Racing in New England*. Bloomington, IN: Xlibris Corporation LLC, 2010.

Triplett, Ken. "Ken Triplett's Racing History." Accessed July 5, 2014. http://triplettracehistory.blogspot.com/2014/04/bill-endicott-racing-on-alone-bill.html.

Youngblood, Ed. "Moto History." Accessed July 5, 2014. http://www.motohistory.net/news2007/news-feb07.html.

ABOUT THE AUTHOR

*A*manda Becker was born and raised and continues to live in Rockford. She graduated from Rockford Auburn High School in 2000 and earned her associate's degree from Rock Valley College in 2002 and her bachelor's degree in history from Rockford College (now Rockford University) in 2005. After she graduated from Rockford College, she returned to her alma mater, Auburn High School, to teach social science courses, and she continues to do so today. In addition to teaching at Auburn, she is involved in many community organizations, such as Midway Village, the Rockford Historical Society, Haunted Rockford tours and the Rock Valley College Center for Learning in Retirement (CLR).

Visit us at
www.historypress.com